ORCHIDS

BY PETER ARNOLD

RIZZOLI
NEW YORK

'ESPECIALLY FOR AARON'

ACKNOWLEDGMENTS

MY THANKS TO: Terry, Jean, and Russell Cook at Ivens Orchids,
Brian and Sara Rittershausen at Burnham Nurseries Ltd., Jim and
Lauris Rose at Cal Orchid Inc., Jan and Ian Plested at Plested Orchids,
Bob Dadd at Greenaway Orchids, Barry Findon, Barry Tattersall,
Dr. Gustav A.L. Mehlquist

MY SPECIAL THANKS TO: Elizabeth Dowle for her beautiful illustrations. Rosie Claxton, Stella Dillon, Jackie Smithson, Kay Runyon,
Lori Rand, Betsy Porter, and Maurice Hyams for their support
and encouragement, and Rick Runyon for his production assistance.
And lastly, Piak Suchart Lakdee.

First published in the United States of America in 1994 by
Rizzoli International Publications, Inc.
300 Park Avenue South, New York, NY 10010
Reprinted 2002

Library of Congress Cataloging-in-Publication Data

Arnold, Peter, 1946–
Orchids / Peter Arnold.
p.   cm.
Includes index.
ISBN 0-8478-1810-1
1. Orchids. 2. Orchid culture. 3. Orchids—Pictorial works.
I. Title.
SB409.A76 1994
635.9'3415   93-49405   CIP

Design by Steven Schoenfelder
Printed in Italy

TITLE PAGE
Miltoniopsis Celle
(syn. *Miltonia* Celle)
X/I (*Milt.* Lydia x *Milt.* Lingwood)

CONTENTS

FOREWORD AND PHOTOGRAPHIC NOTES

I obtained my first orchid as a house plant some ten years ago, and I was excited and enthused by its exotic flowers and their intoxicating perfume. It was a glorious *Oncidium* with flowers in shades of pink and purple; not the more familiar *Cattleya* bloom associated with wedding corsages. The plant had a profusion of buds, and flowered for many weeks, filling the room with a lingering fragrance each morning. Unfortunately, when the flowers died away, I did not take the trouble to find out how to care for the plant. I watered it from time to time when it seemed too dry, but it did not flower again the next season, and was relegated to the back of my greenhouse, leaving me with the impression that orchids were difficult to care for and rather temperamental. It was not until several years later, when I was introduced to a couple who owned an orchid nursery, that I started keeping orchids at home again. This time I learned more about their cultivation requirements and was rewarded with success. I became captivated by the allure of these extraordinary plants and their beautiful and sensuous blooms.

There is a certain mystery about orchids, and many keen gardeners who are accomplished with other plants are intimidated and shy away from growing them. It is a common misconception that all orchids come from hot steamy jungles and are therefore very difficult to grow in more temperate areas. The orchid family consists of some thirty thousand natural species growing in the wild, and is the most varied and highly evolved family of the entire plant kingdom. The orchid's natural habitat extends from the tropical zones of the equator through to the Arctic Circle, and from regions at sea level to mountainous altitudes. Therefore, there are now cultivated orchids available to suit almost every environment. It is important, however, to give each particular orchid variety conditions that resemble the plant's natural environment as closely as possible in terms of light, humidity, and temperature. If these basic requirements are fulfilled, you will enjoy a flourishing plant that produces beautiful flowers. Most orchids are not as fragile as one might believe; they are quite sturdy and resilient and will withstand a certain amount of mistreatment. The blooms of many popular orchids can outlast those of most other houseplants, and remain fresh for many weeks, and sometimes months, whether on the plant or in a vase. Many varieties have been commercially hybridized to tolerate artificial conditions and suit household environments.

I am now an avid orchid enthusiast and have grown many different orchids, both species and hybrids, and I have entered my orchids in flower shows and competitions. It was an obvious choice, therefore, for me to follow the success of my recent book, *Tulips*, with a similar photographic study of orchids and their flowers. I have tried not only to include strikingly colored hybrids, but also unfamiliar species. I found that photographing orchids was completely different from my experience with tulips, and they presented much more of a challenge. Some orchids grow like regular potted plants, while others are vines many meters long; still others are of minuscule proportions. Many orchids support luxuriant foliage, and others have no leaves at all. But they all produce interesting and unusual flowers, some beautiful and some bizarre.

In my photographs, I have tried to capture the uniqueness and aesthetic beauty of the orchid family, and the endless variety of extraordinary flowers. I used artificial light to bring out specific textures and characteristics of individual flowers. I posed them against either black or white backgrounds to give the flowers more impact and to accentuate their graphic form. I used an electronic flash unit with a single flash-head light source on the subject, in conjunction with black felt, to obtain black backgrounds. To achieve clean white backgrounds, I used an extra flash-head directed onto a white paper backdrop. My camera is a Hasselblad 500 CM 6cm x 6cm and I used 80mm as well as 150mm Sonar lenses, sometimes in conjunction with extension tubes or proxars, for very close-up or macro shots. Most of the photographs were exposed at aperture f. 16 to give optimum depth of field and sharpness to the images. I usually bracket the exposures half an f-stop to each side of the metered light readings to obtain perfect exposure and precise color renditions. I chose Fuji 120mm film to bring out reds and yellows, and Kodak film for other color

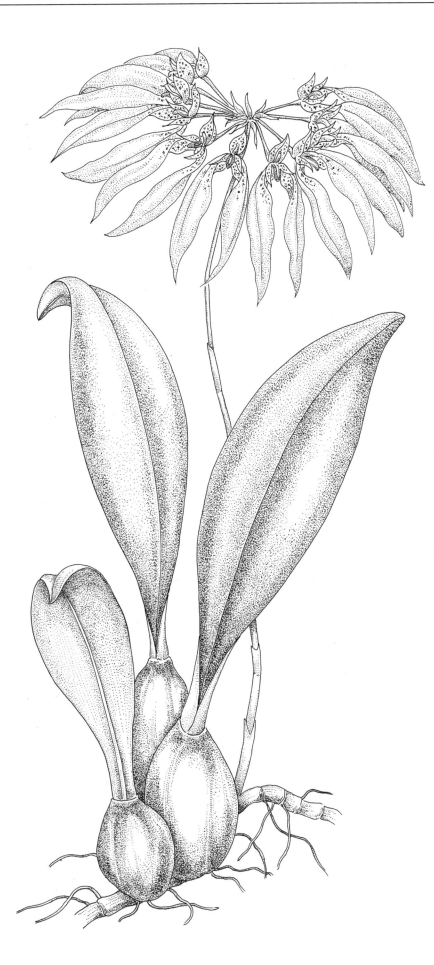

registers. My exhibition prints are made on Ilfordchrome Classic paper and Fuji Ultragloss.

Many of my pictures were taken in California and Florida, but I also traveled to New York and Canada. When I heard that particular varieties had come into flower, I took my photographic equipment on location with me and set up at the nursery, or when I was allowed to borrow the plant, in my hotel room. Other photographs were taken in England, which supports a thriving enclave of orchid enthusiasts and societies, and specialist orchid nurseries that rival any in the world. I also visited the orchid farms of Thailand, which, because of its enormous cut flower industry, is the country perhaps most associated with orchids, and I concluded my travels with a trip to Singapore, where the national flower is the natural hybrid *Vanda* Miss Joaquim, illustrated on the back cover.

Everyone was very helpful and enthusiastic about my endeavors. This photographic project has given me a great deal of pleasure and the research has broadened my knowledge and understanding of orchids. I hope that this book will dispel any trepidations readers might have about orchids, and give them the inspiration to have a go at growing these wonderful plants themselves.

Cirrhopetalum picturatum
(syn. Bulbophyllum picturatum)
S/H

THE HISTORY OF ORCHIDS

EARLY HISTORY

The history of orchids in Europe is well documented and early references can be traced to the ancient Greeks, who called them *Orchis* and *Satyrion*. In his manuscript, *Enquiry Into Plants*, the Greek philosopher Theophrastus (372–287 B.C., a pupil of Aristotle) refers to a group of Mediterranean *Orchis* plants, whose roots were dried, chopped, and used in medicine. The modern name 'orchid' is derived from the Greek word *Orchis*, meaning testis, and refers to the plant's underground storage roots, which are testiculate tubers in pairs resembling part of the male sexual anatomy. In Medieval times, medical theories were based on the Doctrine of Signatures, which linked human anatomy to nature. If a plant resembled part of the human body, it was thought to have some remedial or healing effect on the anatomic part it resembled. Therefore, orchid tubers were recommended as an aphrodisiac and used in sexual cures and potions. It was also believed they had magical properties and could determine the sex of an unborn child, providing a male child if eaten by the father, or a female child if eaten by the mother. Early herbalists called orchids *Satyrion*, as they were thought to be the food of satyrs. Legend held that orchids were seedless plants that grew spontaneously from the spilled seminal fluid of mating animals. A great deal of mystery surrounded orchids, and these intriguing myths continued into the seventeenth century. Even today in Greece and the Middle East, orchid tubers are still used to concoct stimulants, anti-depressants, and a nutritious drink called Salep, thought to have aphrodisiac qualities. Vanilla essence, used as a flavoring in ice cream and other foods, is derived from the orchid *Vanilla planifolia*, and long before Europeans discovered America, the ancient Aztecs of Mexico used its seedpods to flavor a traditional drink made from cocoa beans.

In Europe, interest in orchids derived mainly from their medicinal uses, but for many centuries orchids had been appreciated and cultivated in China and the Far East for their aesthetic beauty, not only of the flowers but also of the leaves. Confucius (551–479 B.C.) praised the beauty and fragrance of imperial orchids twenty-five hundred years ago, and mentioned them in the *I-Ching*. The species revered in the East were mainly the small-flowered terrestrial *Cymbidium* and it is recorded that *Cymbidium ensifolium* has been cultivated in China for more than two thousand years.

THE INTRODUCTION OF TROPICAL ORCHIDS TO EUROPE

The seventeenth century was an important time of European colonization, when seafaring expeditions journeyed to all corners of the world in quest of new lands and new trade routes. These expeditions returned with curiosities and artifacts that had never before been seen in Europe, including unusual tropical plants, which were collected and brought back as botanical oddities. Early research into flora and fauna was conducted by the physicians employed by trading companies. Later, when missionaries and churchmen were sent to spread Christianity in the new lands, they were fascinated by local flora and continued the work of recording endemic plant life.

During the seventeenth century, the West Indies had become an important base for foreign trade, and there were regular sailings between Europe and the Caribbean. Although the tropical Americas had previously been discovered and colonized by the Spanish and Portuguese, there seems to be little evidence that these explorers sent any orchids except *Vanilla* back to Europe. The first recorded tropical orchid to flower in England arrived in 1731 from the Bahamas. It was the terrestrial species *Bletia verecunda*, sent to a cloth merchant, Peter Collinson, and later acquired by Sir Charles Wager. This unusual botanical specimen with bright magenta blooms was quite unlike any of the familiar European orchids and triggered widespread interest. Naval officers and explorers were encouraged to bring back more orchid plants from tropical regions, both as botanical specimens and as gifts for their ladies. Attempts were made in England and other northern European countries to cultivate orchids, but with limited success. In an effort to simulate jungle conditions, special hothouses were built with solid walls, allowing very little light or ventilation, two of the main requisites

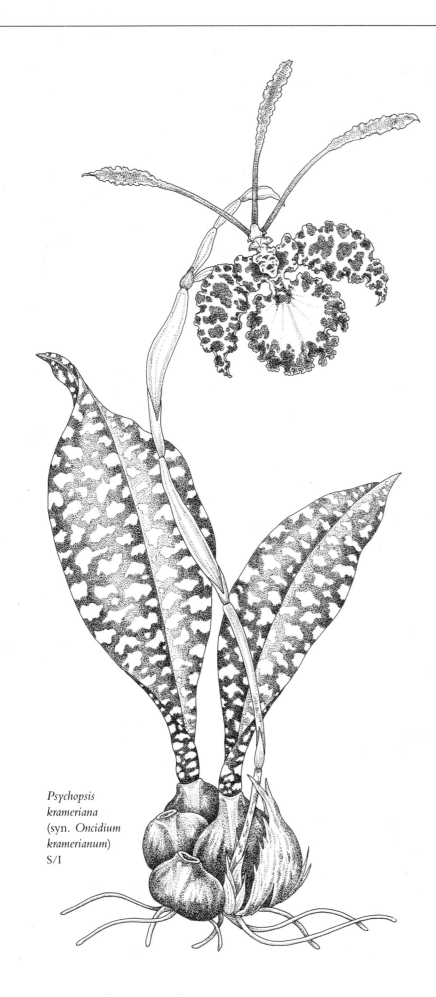

Psychopsis
krameriana
(syn. *Oncidium*
kramerianum)
S/I

for orchids to flourish. The plants were subjected to excessive heat and high humidity in these hothouses, which were eventually dubbed 'stoves'. Very few orchids survived these stifling conditions.

The eighteenth century was an era of research and learning, and a more enlightened approach to botany. Outdated medicinal practices originating in myth and superstition were replaced by more scientific knowledge. In 1737, the Swedish Botanist, Carl von Linné (usually referred to as Linnaeus) made the first attempt at a systematic classification of plants in his work *Genera Plantarum*. Until this time, the names of most plants were long Latin phrases, but he introduced a binomial system of nomenclature, using only two names in Latin to describe each plant. This basic system is still in use today. By 1763, Linnaeus had collated over one hundred different orchid species, a clue to the number of native and imported plants known at the time to botanists and private collectors. ·

New tropical orchid plants continued to hold great interest as curiosities for botanists and a few wealthy plant enthusiasts. Until the second half of the century, most orchids came from the West Indies, but plant collecting expeditions were now encouraged to explore other parts of the world. In 1768, under the auspices of the Royal Society, James Cook and Joseph Banks embarked upon an expedition for botanical exploration to the South Seas and Australia. Further plant collecting expeditions were initiated, and in 1778 Dr. John Fothergill, an English physician, returned from China with the first Asiatic orchids, including *Limodorum grandiflorum* (now known as *Phaius tankervilleae*; common name, Nun's orchid) and *Cymbidium ensifolium*. In 1780, Joseph Banks, who had become a noted explorer and naturalist, brought the first orchids to England from Australia. He later received a baronetcy for his services to horticulture and helped to found the Royal Horticultural Society in 1804. In 1793, the infamous Captain Bligh of the well known 'Mutiny on the Bounty' saga, made an expedition to South America in HMS *Providence* and returned with more exotic orchids, including *Epidendrum, Oncidium*, and *Lycaste*. In England, horticulture flourished through the collaboration of amateur enthusiasts and professional botanists, and as a result of their interest in their interest in botanical discovery, the Royal Botanical Gardens at Kew were conceived. By this time, certain tropical orchids were fairly common in Europe, and there had been some success with cultivating them. By 1789, records show fifteen different tropical orchids in cultivation at Kew, including *Encyclia fragrans* and *Encyclia cochleata* (page 27), which first flowered in England in 1787, but was then known as *Epidendrum cochleatum*.

This was also a period of trade and prosperity when many of the great houses of Europe were built. Formal gardens were designed on the grounds of these houses, and gardening and plants became an important part of the aristocratic way of life. Tropical orchids were showy and colorful, quite unlike any European flowers, and the aristocracy were keen to obtain these unusual specimens and put them on display in their hothouses. When new species came into flower for the first time, it was exciting news and was reported in newspapers and periodicals. However, no one knew exactly what conditions they required to grow successfully. Orchids were still shrouded in mystery, and it was generally thought that there was something sinister about them. They seemed to defy the laws of nature. It was said that they did not grow in soil, but on trees, their roots strangling the branches and trunks; hence the misconception that they were parasites. It was also claimed that they were used in fertility ceremonies by natives, and that they were carnivorous, devouring insects for nourishment. Exciting tales spread regarding each new orchid discovery. These stories caught the imagination of the aristocracy, and the more outrageous the story associated with a particular orchid, the greater became the demand for the plant.

EARLY CULTIVATION

In 1812, Conrad Loddiges of Hackney, London began a commercial orchid operation that catered to the increasing demand for orchids, and in 1815 he experimented in growing orchids by unorthodox methods. Rather than suffocating the plants in hothouse conditions, he still kept them under glass, but placed them in well-ventilated areas and watered them frequently. They responded favorably to this treatment and news spread about his success. Other growers followed suit and tried new methods of cultivation.

In November of 1818, the first *Cattleya* flowered in Europe and created a sensation. The plant had been sent to England as dried packing material in a consignment of tropical plants from Brazil, and one of the first amateur growers, William Cattley, succeeded in growing it. No one had ever seen an orchid like it in cultivation—with its large, flamboyant flowers and elaborate trumpet-like 'lip'. Dr. John Lindley, Professor of Botany at the University of London and Secretary to the Royal Horticultural Society, named it *Cattleya labiata-autumnalis* in honor of Cattley, and referring to the flower's unusual 'lip' and the fact that it flowered in autumn. Demand for this spectacular flower was so great that orchids became big business almost overnight, prompting rampant collecting in South America to obtain every possible specimen.

John Lindley edited *The Gardener's Chronicle* and wrote extensively about orchids and their cultivation. In 1830, he presented a paper recommending that certain orchids be grown in cooler, humid conditions. This advice was good for species from rainforests at high altitudes, but most tropical orchids in cultivation at that time were from warmer lowland areas. Enthusiasts applied his advice to all orchids, with unfortunate consequences, and thousands of irreplaceable plants perished. Lindley later corresponded with orchid hobbyists throughout the world and collated information on the habitats and climatic conditions in which orchids grew in the wild, ascertaining that orchids from various origins grew in different climatic conditions. His findings were published in *The Gardener's Chronicle* and in the *Botanical Registrar* and eventually led to more successful methods of growing orchids.

THE ORCHID HUNTERS

Until the early nineteenth century, orchids were collected by hobbyists and sent back to Europe with other trade merchandise. But as the orchid craze swept through Europe, these amateurs were ousted by aggressive professional orchid hunters, sponsored by wealthy benefactors and astute businessmen who were only interested in large financial returns. Some embarked on expeditions without any knowledge of the conditions they were likely to encounter and were completely unprepared for impenetrable jungle, dense rainforests, unfriendly natives, and often debilitating or fatal tropical diseases that had never before been encountered by Europeans. Many of these orchid hunters were pushed to the limits of their endurance and never returned—but the tales of their misfortune and disaster only reinforced the popular interest in orchids.

There was great competition and rivalry among collectors, and they became ruthless and cunning in their efforts to ensure the rarity of particular orchids. The locations of certain prized plants were shrouded in secrecy, and unscrupulous collectors deliberately gave misleading reports of the geographic origins of new discoveries. (A side-effect of this practice was poor cultivation techniques back in Europe, which were based on the misleading information on the plants' environments.) Tens of thousands of specimens of individual orchid species were collected in order to exhaust the source and therefore obtain exclusive control of particular species. Unfortunately, conservation was not the important issue it is today. Enormous tracts of jungle were stripped of certain rare orchids, and forests were pillaged and burned, resulting in the extinction of the many species of flora and fauna that remained. Vast consignments were sent to England on a regular basis. The plants were first hacked from their treetop clingholds with machetes, then dried out and packed into crates and barrels and transported by pack animals or native bearers to a riverbank to await shipment. Often the boat did not arrive for weeks, and dampness and disease set into the consignment. Once on board, the plants were stored in stuffy holds, without light or air. They had to endure sea journeys of three to four months on sailing ships before arriving at their destination. Most plants were found dead on arrival, and the supply was never enough to meet the extraordinary demand.

Between 1830 and 1834, Nathaniel Ward perfected closed wooden and glass cases for shipping plants from far-off lands. This helped a great many more orchids reach their destinations alive. Ward's contribution to orchid culture was recognized and his name is perpetuated in the names of several orchids, including *Stanhopea wardii*. Today, similar glass display cases are called Wardian cases.

Existing plant nurseries soon realized the opportunity to make large profits by supplying the ever-increasing demand for new orchid species, and commercial horticulturalists in Great Britain, France, Germany, and Belgium joined the orchid trade. Messrs. James Veitch and Son, of Exeter, and later Chelsea in England, became the first commercial nurserymen to employ orchid collectors, and many new species were discovered as a result of their endeavors. Collector Thomas Lobb was sent to Java in 1843, India in 1848, and subsequently to the Philippines. By 1850, collectors had penetrated the Andes of South America and introduced cooler-growing species. The orchid industry was spurred on by demand, and collectors were sent in droves to all parts of the globe to search out new species. They ventured to Africa, Borneo, Indonesia, and eventually New Guinea. The exotic orchid trade reached its peak in the late 1850s and flourished until the turn of the century.

A few plant collectors became very wealthy, and those who were most successful were immortalized in the names of the orchids they discovered. Among these collectors were Joseph von Warscewicz (*Miltonioides warscewiczii*, page 54), who made several trips to Central and South America and brought back *Miltonia* and *Cattleya,* and Gustave Wallis, who collected many new species from Ecuador and Colombia.

VICTORIAN "ORCHIDMANIA"

Orchids became fashionable status objects in Victorian England, and the overwhelming demand for orchids in the Victorian era typifies the excesses of the period. "Orchidmania" gripped England, similar to Holland's "Tulipmania" of the seventeenth century. Orchids were regarded as novel curiosities rather than plants. It was not only the flowers that captured imaginations, but also the challenge of coaxing the plants to produce blooms. Until the 1840s, most orchids sent back to Europe were tropical lowland species requiring high temperatures, and only the wealthy could afford the heating for their cultivation. Those who were wealthy enough bought all the orchids they could obtain and built conservatories, or 'crystal palaces' as they became known, to house them. One of the finest collections was started by the wealthy and extravagant William George Spencer Cavendish, the sixth Duke of Devonshire. He lavished a fortune on his relentless pursuit to discover new exotic orchid species, sending collectors to Brazil, South America, and later to Mexico, Guatemala, Malaya, and Assam in India. Under the supervision of his head gardener, Joseph Paxton, he built an enormous conservatory covering nearly an acre of garden at Chatsworth House, and within a decade he had amassed the largest private orchid collection in the world.

Joseph Paxton is probably best remembered for designing the conservatory at Crystal Palace in London, for which he was knighted. In 1845, Britain's glass tax was repealed, making glasshouses more affordable and accelerating the growth of the orchid industry. Paxton was keen for amateurs to have the opportunity to cultivate orchids and developed the idea of mass-producing glass panels, frames, and struts to make smaller glasshouses available to ordinary people. He contributed a great deal to orchid cultivation and was partly responsible for perpetuating public interest in orchids. He experimented with different orchids and discovered that most orchids require a moist atmosphere, and that healthy flowers depend on healthy roots. He also ascertained that many showy orchids from the tropics and sub-tropics grew on mountain slopes and preferred cooler growing conditions. Paxton urged that species from the higher altitudes of Mexico and elsewhere should be collected and made available to amateurs of limited means. These orchids did not require artificial heating, and the lower expense involved in growing these plants made them popular. In *The Gardener's Chronicle*, Benjamin S. Williams wrote a famous series of articles entitled "Orchids for the Millions," which met with immediate success and became the basis for *The Orchid Grower's Manual*, which in turn proved to be so popular that it was reprinted seven times during his lifetime, and many times since.

Instead of being accessible to only a few privileged and wealthy enthusiasts, orchid cultivation was transformed into a hobby that everyone could enjoy.

At the height of "Orchidmania" in 1876, Frederick Sander established a famous nursery at St. Albans in Hertfordshire, England and sponsored expeditions to the Phillipines, Borneo, and the Andes. By 1894, records confirm he had twenty collectors searching for new orchid species. He enjoyed a great deal of success as his collectors discovered many fine orchids, including *Phalaenopsis sanderiana, Paphiopedilum sanderianum, Vanda sanderiana*, and many others which were named after him. He later established the largest known commercial orchid nursery, covering thirty acres in Bruges, Belgium, to supply the European market, and he employed collectors until 1914. His success earned him the nickname "The Orchid King," and he was appointed Royal Orchid Grower by Queen Victoria.

During this era, auction sales were organized in England at Covent Garden, Kings Street, and the Stevens' Auction Rooms, and also in Belgium. They were attended with excitement and enthusiasm, and rare orchids sold for incredible sums. Single plant specimens sold for over one hundred pounds and there are records of a *Cattleya* selling for over six hundred pounds. A particularly fine specimen of *Odontoglossum crispum,* 'Frederick Sander,' sold for over fifteen hundred pounds. The furor spread throughout Europe and culminated in the International Exhibition in Brussels, Belgium, for which specimens were specially collected and transported from Singapore and other exotic locations.

ORCHID CULTIVATION IN THE UNITED STATES AND ASIA

While orchid fever was rampant in Europe, interest also developed in the United States. The first exotic orchids were sent to John Boott of Massachusetts in 1838 by his brother, who lived in London, and by the middle of the nineteenth century, many more had arrived in America. Several notable collections were established in the English tradition, mainly in the New England region. In 1865, the collection of Edward Rand was presented to Harvard University and housed at the Cambridge Botanical Gardens. Harvard's collection is still considered very important in the world of orchids.

When the First World War broke out, many European collections were destroyed or perished, mainly because of lack of fuel to heat the greenhouses. These losses did not occur in the United States, and the popularity of private orchid collections continued to grow. Famous collections such as the Du Pont Estate at Longwood Gardens in Delaware, and the Missouri Botanical Gardens in St. Louis, Missouri, are open for public viewing today.

As a result of the war, English firms no longer had collectors throughout the world, and importation of orchids into England almost ceased. The Second World War brought further disaster to those orchid collections that had survived in Europe, and the industry virtually collapsed. However, the collection at Kew Gardens survived and still continues to grow. Several hundred species are cultivated there today, and it is probably the oldest surviving collection anywhere in the world. The two world wars shifted the center of orchid culture from Europe to the United States, especially to California and Florida, where the climate is more conducive to orchid growing.

Immediately after World War II, interest in growing orchids also began to develop among a few wealthy hobbyists in Thailand. Gradually, orchid growing became commercially viable, and an active export industry evolved that eventually expanded to cater to the international cut flower market. In 1980, when European countries were feeling the effects of the oil crisis and cutting down on imports, Thailand diversified and developed its potted orchid industry to supply the Japanese market. The Japanese grew these plants for a further one or two years, then resold them. Thailand then began transporting orchid flowers by air, opening up the cut flower industry to the United States. This increased orchid sales in Thailand and Singapore, and today orchid sprays are air-freighted from Asia to flower shops all over the globe. Many other countries are now looking to the flower trade as a source of revenue, and the orchid industry is currently worth many millions of dollars to developing countries.

KEY TO PHOTOGRAPH CAPTION SYMBOLS	
hybrid information	greenhouse information
PX=primary hybrid	H=hot house
X=hybrid	I=intermediate house
S=species	C=cool house

PHOTOGRAPHS

LEFT
Dendrobium thyrsiflorum
(Den. densiflorum var. alboluteum)
Burmese orchid
S/I

ABOVE
Comparettia speciosa
S/C

LEFT
Phalaenopsis Golden Emperor 'Sweet'
FCC/AOS
X/H (*Phal.* Snow Daffodil x *Phal.*
Mambo)

ABOVE
Cymbidium Goldrun 'Cooksbridge'
X/C (*Cym.* Cariga x *Cym.*
Runnymede)

OVERLEAF LEFT
Phragmipedium besseae
S/I

OVERLEAF RIGHT
Masdevallia Falcata AM/AOS
PX/C (*M. coccinea* x *M. veitchiana*)

Coelogyne Burfordiense
Black orchid
PX/H (*Coel. asperata* x *Coel.*
pandurata)

ABOVE
Encyclia cochleata
(syn. *Epidendrum cochleatum*)
Cockleshell orchid
S/I

OVERLEAF LEFT
Miltonia Santa Barbara 'Rainbow
Swirl'
Pansy orchid
X/I (*Milt.* Alan Iseri x *Milt.*
Limelight)

OVERLEAF RIGHT
Paphiopedilum Magic Lantern
PX/I (*Paph. micranthum* x *Paph.*
delenati)

ABOVE
Ophrys holoserica
(syn. *O. fuciflora*)
Late Spider orchid
S/C

RIGHT
Vanda Rothschildiana
(syn. *Vandanthe* Rothschildiana)
PX/H (*V. coerulea* x *V. sanderiana*)

OVERLEAF LEFT
Coryanthes speciosa
Bucket orchid
S/I

ABOVE
Lycaste deppei
(syn. *Maxillaria deppei*)
S/I

30

LEFT

Dendrobium lasianthera
S/H

ABOVE

Trichoglottis philippensis var. brachiata
(syn. *Trgl. brachiata*)
S/H

OVERLEAF LEFT

Cymbidium Pure Bisque
X/C (*Cym.* Melinga x *Cym.* Pharaoh)

OVERLEAF RIGHT

Rhyncholaelia digbyana
(syn. *Brassavola digbyana*)
S/I

ABOVE
Catasetum Susan Fuchs
X/I (**Ctsm. expansum** x **Ctsm.**
Orchidglade)

RIGHT
Anguloa clowesii
Tulip orchid, Cradle orchid
S/I

OVERLEAF LEFT
Renanthera monachica 'Highcliffe
Castle'
S/H

OVERLEAF RIGHT
Psychopsis krameriana
(syn. **Oncidium kramerianum**)
S/I

42

Above
Cattleya Interglossa
PX/I (*C. amethystoglossa* x *C. intermedia*)

Overleaf Left
Cymbidium elegans
S/C

Overleaf Right
Cycnoches ventricosum var. chlorochilon
(syn. *Cycnoches chlorochilon*)
Swan orchid
S/I

ABOVE
Cyrtochilum macranthum
(syn. *Oncidium macranthum*)
S/I

RIGHT
Odontoglossum Yellow Alba
X/C (*Odm.* Golden Rialto x *Odm.*
Pancho)

OVERLEAF LEFT
Ascocenda Blue Boy
X/H (*Ascda.* Meda Arnold x *V.*
coerulea)

OVERLEAF RIGHT
Dactylorhiza fuchsii
Marsh orchid
S/C

LEFT
Miltassia Aztec 'Nalo' HCC/AOS
X/I (*Mtssa.* Cartagena x *Milt.* Minas
Gerais)
Miltassia = (*Miltonia* x *Brassia*)

ABOVE
Cirrhopetalum eberhardtii
(syn. *Bulbophyllum eberhardtii*)
S/H

OVERLEAF LEFT
Lycaste Auburn
X/I (*Lyc.* Balliae x *Lyc.* Sunrise)

OVERLEAF RIGHT
Disa uniflora
Pride of Table Mountain
S/C

LEFT
Cirrhopetalum graveolens
(syn. *Bulbophyllum graveolens*)
S/H

ABOVE
Cymbidium Fort George 'Lewes'
AM/RHS
X/C (*Cym.* Baltic x *Cym.* York
Meradith)

OVERLEAF
Odontoglossum La Ponterrin
X/C (*Odm. rossii* x *Odm.* Panise)

ABOVE
Ophrys kotschyi
(syn. *Ophrys cypria*)
S/C

RIGHT
Paphiopedilum bellatulum
S/I

OVERLEAF LEFT
Eriopsis biloba 'Highcliffe Castle'
AM/RHS
S/I

OVERLEAF RIGHT
Phragmipedium caudatum var.
warscewiczianum
(syn. *Phragmipedium warscewiczianum*)
Mandarin orchid
S/I

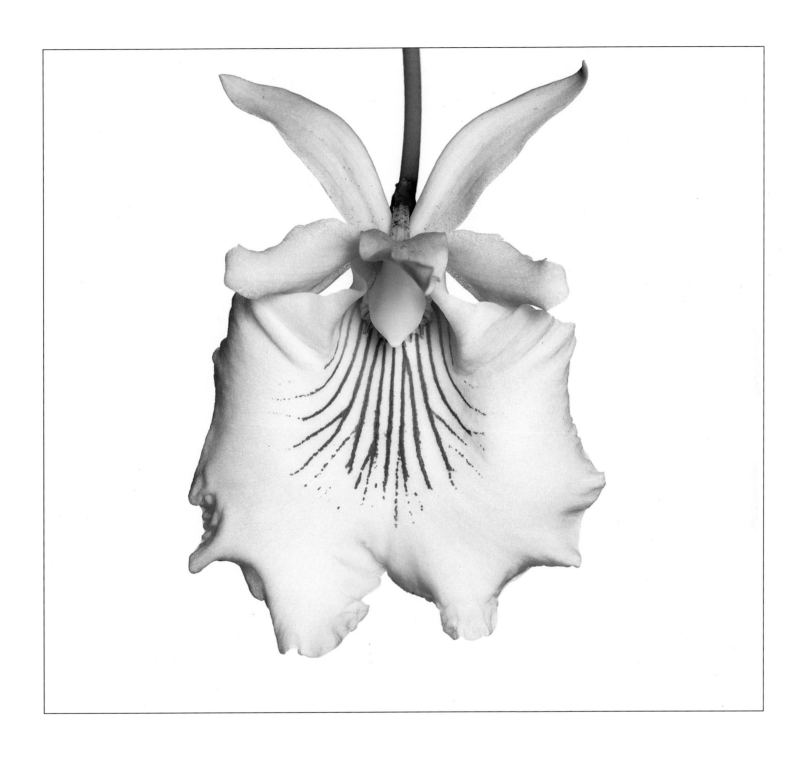

ABOVE
Cochleanthes amazonica Marshmallow
HCC/AOS
S/I

OVERLEAF LEFT
Brassoepidendrum Pseudosa
X/I (*B. nodosa* x *Epi.*
pseudepidendrum)
Brassoepidendrum= (*Brassavola* x
Epidendrum)

OVERLEAF RIGHT
Brassocattleya Jean Murray 'Allen
Christenson'
X/I (*Bc.* Déesse x *C.* Margaret
Stewart)

ABOVE
Oncidium (*Onc.* Fall Delight x *Onc.* Sultmyre)
Dancing Lady orchid
X/C

RIGHT
Laeliocattleya Little Pete
X/I (*C. aurantiaca* x *L.* Icarus)

OVERLEAF LEFT
Brassia Rex 'Sakata'
PX/I (*Brs. verrucosa* x *Brs. gireoudiana*)

OVERLEAF RIGHT
Paphiopedilum malipoense
Slipper orchid
S/I

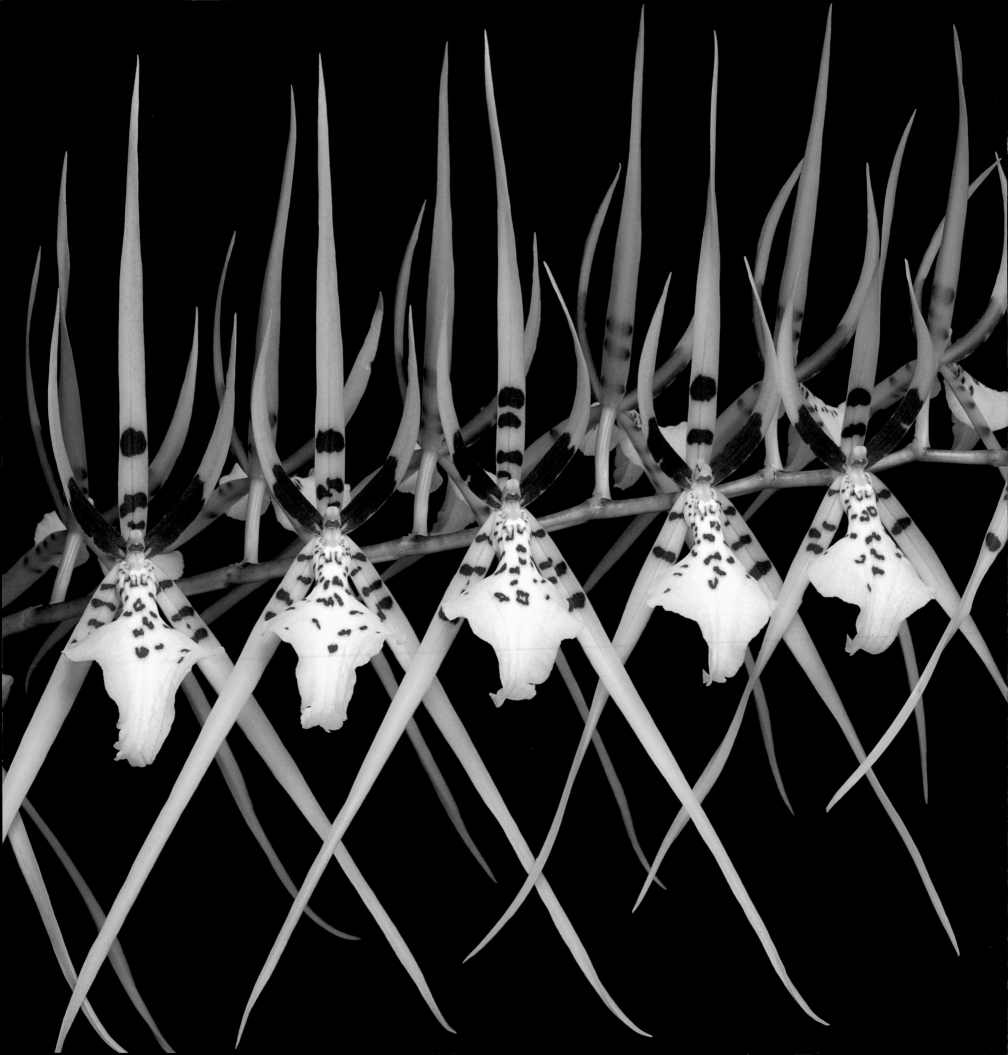

ABOVE
Phalaenopsis lueddemanniana var.
pulchra
(syn. *Phalaenopsis pulchra*)
S/H

RIGHT
Dendrobium Waipahu Beauty
X/H (*Den*. Theodore Takiguchi x
Den. Lady Hamilton)

OVERLEAF
Masdevallia constricta
(syn. *Masdevallia urosalpinx*)
S/C

BOTANICAL TRAITS OF
THE ORCHID FAMILY

Orchids are perennial flowering plants belonging to the scientific family ORCHIDACEAE. It is the largest flowering plant family, and consists of some thirty thousand species and more than eighty thousand hybrids. Orchids grow in nearly every country of the world, except in Arctic regions, and in almost every climate except deserts and permanent snowcaps. Over a third of the world's orchids derive from the tropical and sub-tropical regions of Central and South America, while the temperate regions of North America and Canada have comparatively few endemic species. There are between one hundred fifty and two hundred natural species in North America, and probably the same number in Europe, fifty of which are native to the British Isles. Orchids vary so much in terms of growth habits, form, size, and color, that it is often difficult to believe that they all come from the same family. In spite of their amazing variety, however, all orchids do have certain common characteristics that enable botanists to distinguish them from other plants.

For practical purposes, orchids are generally classified into two categories: epiphytes and terrestrials. Most tropical orchids are EPIPHYTES (from the Latin *epi*-upon, and *phyte*-plant) and grow on branches or on the trunks of trees, with their long aerial roots dangling freely, giving them the name 'air plants'. In the early days of botanical research, the fact that epiphytic orchids grow without soil inspired the belief that they were parasites, deriving their nutrition from the plants on which they grew. They actually utilize host trees as anchors, clinging to them only for support, while their roots absorb moisture from the air and nutrients from decaying matter on the branches. Epiphytes have developed certain characteristic features associated with their habitats. In tropical rainforests, heavy rain may fall every day, but due to the heat, the moisture soon evaporates. The orchids' roots are covered in a silvery, spongy tissue called VELAMEN, made up of dead cells, that protects the sensitive inner tissue from strong sunlight, exposing only the green root tips. Most epiphytes are accustomed to surviving periods of drought, and as a result, many species have developed swollen stems and fleshy, succulent leaves to assist with water retention.

Occasionally, epiphytes are found growing on rocks or on moist cliff faces, and then are more correctly named LITHOPHYTES(from the Latin *litho*-stone and *phyte*-plant).

TERRESTRIAL orchids (from the Latin *terrestis*-growing on the ground) are mainly found in temperate zones, and tropical grasslands and marshes. They include many species found in the United States, such as *Cypripedium* and all the species native to the British Isles. They obtain their nourishment from minerals and moisture in the ground and photosynthesize through their leaves like other herbaceous plants. Some support a well-developed system of fine root hair that filters nutrients and stabilizes the plant, a characteristic not found in epiphytic and lithophytic orchids. Terrestrial orchids may have to survive periods of adverse weather such as drought or freezing conditions, and many produce swollen underground storage organs similar to tubers from which new shoots grow when weather conditions improve.

A few orchids that live on the forest floor are more correctly named SAPROPHYTES (from the Greek *sapros*-to rot, and *phyte*-plant). Some have no leaves and do not function through photosynthesis. They derive all their nourishment from decaying organic matter through their association with mycorrhiza fungus, which breaks down organic matter for absorption by the plant's roots. Two rare Australian orchids of this type, *Cryphanthemis* and *Rhizanthella*, are almost subterranean, living completely underground except when their tiny flowers push up and appear above the surface.

Orchids produce new growth and enlarge each year by one of two systems of growth: sympodial or monopodial. SYMPODIAL (from the Greek *sym*-united, and *podo*- foot) growth is the way by which certain orchids such as *Cattleya* develop a new growing tip from the base of the previous years' growth and creep forward each year (see illustration, page 98), sometimes underground, but usually above the surface. This growth is similar to a rhizome and often has several branches, each of which produces a new shoot. In most sympodial orchids, the new shoot swells and develops into a reserve storage organ like a tuber to store water and nutrients in time of

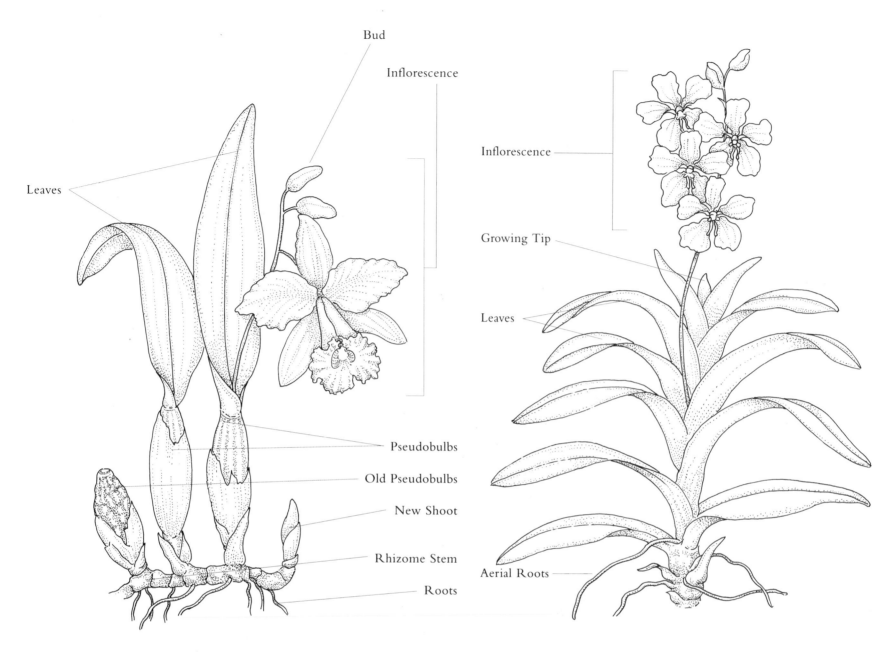

Bud

Inflorescence

Leaves

Inflorescence

Growing Tip

Leaves

Pseudobulbs

Old Pseudobulbs

New Shoot

Rhizome Stem

Roots

Aerial Roots

Sympodial orchid, *Cattleya*

Monopodial orchid, *Vanda*

drought. This is called a PSEUDOBULB, and may either be formed close to the previous years' growth, or spaced further along the developing stem, depending on the species. The new pseudobulb matures and develops all in one season, producing foliage and flowers. The following season, similar growth develops from the dormant bud at the base of the last pseudobulb and the plant progresses forward. While old pseudobulbs may bear leaves, as a general rule only the new season's pseudobulbs bear flowers. The flower spikes may appear from the top, the base, or the side of the pseudobulb depending on the species. Pseudobulbs vary in shape and size, and range from stalk-like stems as in the case of certain *Dendrobium*, to large, swollen bulbs typified by *Cymbidium, Lycaste*, and

Odontoglossum. In the case of *Grammatophyllum speciosum* (Tiger orchid), which is considered to be the largest of orchids, the cylindrical stems resemble sugar cane or bamboo, and can grow to more than three meters tall. Sympodial orchid plants seem to be able to survive indefinitely, and some at Kew Gardens are known to be more than one hundred years old. Examples of sympodial orchids are *Cattleya, Coelogyne, Dendrobium, Epidendrum, Lycaste*, and *Oncidium*.

MONOPODIAL (from the Greek *mono*-one and *podo*-a foot) growth emerges from the single apex of the stem, which continues to grow from the terminal bud (see illustration above). The plant has neither rhizomes nor pseudobulbs and the central stem grows upward direction from the top of the previous growth, becoming taller each year. The leaves grow from the main stem, alternately on opposite sides, and the plant may support leaves on the entire length of the stem. In certain conditions when foliage appears only at the top, the lower leaves have usually dried up and fallen off, leaving an exposed, woody stem. Flower spikes and aerial roots may develop anywhere along the stem. Many monopodial orchids sprout auxiliary shoots, which eventually develop their own root systems and can then be separated from the original plant. Typical monopodial orchids include *Vanda* and *Vanilla*, the climbing, vine-like stem of which may reach lengths of more than one hundred feet (30 meters). Less vigorous is *Phalaenopsis*, which has slower and more compact growth.

FOLIAGE

Leaves grow in a wide variety of shapes and sizes, characteristics that are related to natural environments and prevailing climatic conditions. Terrestrial orchids usually support relatively soft thin leaves which require shade, while tropical epiphytic orchids can have thick, leathery leaves to withstand harsh conditions; firm, narrow leaves for protection against direct sunlight; or succulent leaves for water retention.

Certain orchids are admired for their beautiful, gemlike foliage rather than their flowers and these have been given the common name 'Jewel' orchids. They have exquisite and unusual leaves, ranging in color from bright green to rust red, often with veins of contrasting colors. *Ludisa discolor* (syn. *Haemarie discolor*) is perhaps the most popular jewel orchid, together with others belonging to related genera, such as *Macodes sanderiana*, *Anoecto-chilus roxburghii*, and several of the genus *Zeuxine*.

FLOWERS

Orchid flowers vary from the simple form of *Cymbidium* to the extraordinary shape of *Stanhopea*. Most orchids are fertilized by cross-pollination, and all the extraordinary shapes, colors, and markings have specifically evolved to attract the creatures upon which the plants rely for pollination. Once fertilized, the flowers have served their function and quickly fade. For this reason, commercial growers supplying the cut flower trade protect them from random pollination, thereby enhancing the life of the bloom.

Orchids usually flower once a year, producing blooms in various ways. Many species have pendant flowers on long stalks (*Coelogyne* Burfordiense, page 26), while others support a single flower on an upright stalk, as in certain *Paphiopedilum* (page 86).

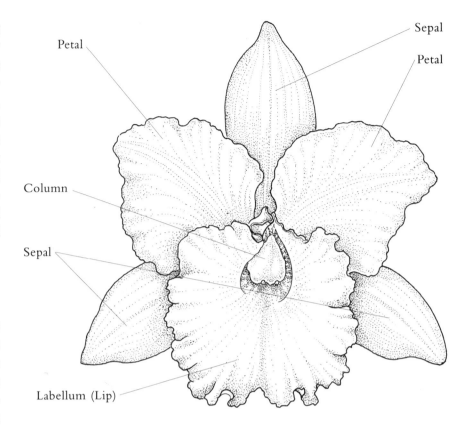

Cattleya, flower structure

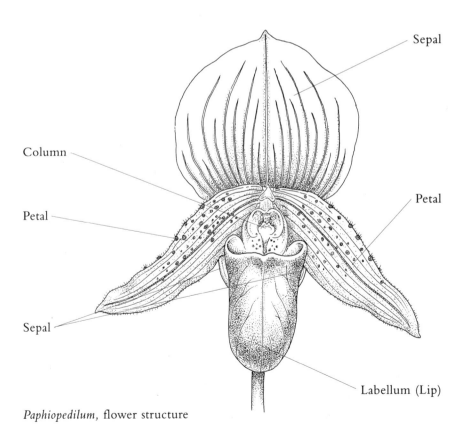

Paphiopedilum, flower structure

Still others may carry up to a hundred blooms on upright stalks or, as in the case of *Renanthera monachica* (page 44), blooms may grow as multi-branched sprays. Flowers may open simultaneously or in succession, and their arrangement on a common stalk is called INFLORESCENCE. The inflorescence is commonly called a spike among orchid growers, and the phrase "in spike" is used to signify that the plant has developed a visible inflorescence which has not yet come into flower. The price of a commercially grown orchid plant is partly based on how many simultaneous flower spikes it produces.

Despite the flowers' complex appearance, the botanical structure of all orchid flowers is very similar. The PERIANTH, or floral envelope, is made up of six basic sections: three outer sepals, and three petals, in addition to a central column that holds the reproductive parts of the plant (see illustrations, page 99). Each flower is attached to the stalk by the pedicel, which extends to the ovary beneath the flower.

The three SEPALS are outer capillary leaves that encase and protect the sexual parts of the flower while the bud develops. In most plants they are green and leaf-like, but in orchids they are more refined and the two lateral sepals usually resemble petals, and are similar to petals in color, shape, and size. However, the sepals are sometimes smaller than the petals and less brightly colored, and the middle, dorsal sepal may be larger and somewhat different in shape. In a few orchids, such as *Masdevallia* (page 57), the sepals are the flower's main feature and the petals are small and insignificant.

Inside the sepals is a set of three PETALS. One of the petals usually differs dramatically from the others, having developed into a lip called the LABELLUM (from the Latin *labium*-meaning lip), and it is this that gives orchid flowers their characteristic appearance. The labellum is one of the main botanical features used to distinguish between species within a single genus. It is usually more conspicuous than the other petals and varies considerably in each genus. It can be unusually large, and is sometimes bigger than all the other flower parts together (page 55), or it can be very much smaller, but it is always distinguishable. Often it is brilliantly marked in two or more colors, spotted, blotched, or striped, and can be frilled, laciniated, or furrowed. All of these characteristics combine to attract pollinators to the center of the flower. In fact, in many orchids, the labellum is located at the top of the forming flower, but before it opens, the pedicel twists one hundred eighty degrees so the labellum is at the bottom to provide a convenient landing stage for visiting pollinators. This process is called RESUPINATION.

The unusual variations of the labellum are especially appealing to orchid enthusiasts, and experimental hybrids are bred to enlarge or accentuate the labellum. The labellum can be convoluted or lobed, and in several European terrestrial orchids, it is uniquely formed in three individual lobes to resemble the forms of insects and other pollinators. The common names of many orchid species originated during Medieval times based on the appearance of the labellum: Man orchid (*Orchis simia*), Lady orchid (*Orchis purpurea*) and Tongue orchid (*Serapias neglecta*, page 18).

The Lady's Slipper orchid has a labellum that forms a receptacle (*Paphiopedilum micranthum*, page 55), and in *Stanhopea Assidensis* (page 69) the labellum is divided into three parts.

The COLUMN is located in the center of the flower, and it is this unique structure of the reproductive organs that distinguishes orchids from other plant families. Instead of having separate male and female sexual parts as in other flowers, the stigma and pistil (the female sexual organs) and the stamen and anther (the male sexual organs) have, through evolution, completely fused together to form a single structure, the column. There is a single anther at the end of the column, attached by a delicate filament, and protected by an anther cap. In most orchids the grains of pollen are assembled to form a waxy mass called the POLLINIUM, located on the anther. Most orchids have two pollinia, although four, or eight are occasionally present, based on the species. Also found in the column is the stigma, usually forming a small sticky hollow into which the pollen from another flower is deposited. Most orchids produce bi-sexual flowers, and can either self-pollinate or cross-pollinate, but in a few species of the genera *Catasetum, Cycnoches*, and *Mormodes,* the plant bears flowers of each sex on different stalks and sometimes also hermaphrodite flowers, all on the same plant. In the wild, fertilization takes place when the pollen from one flower is transferred and deposited on the stigma of another compatible flower, thereby pollinating the second flower. If the second flower is a different species than that from which the pollen has been removed, but is genetically compatible, the result is a natural hybrid. Pollinators include insects, flies, beetles, wasps and bees, moths and butterflies, and even small birds, such as tiny hummingbirds and sunbirds.

The design of the labellum is often a factor in this pollination process, ingeniously working with the structure of the flower to promote pollination. *Coryanthes* are commonly called 'Bucket orchids,' because the labellum looks like a bucket, and is capable of trapping insect pollinators. *Coryanthes speciosa* (page 32) has developed two glands that secrete a syrupy residue that attracts potential pollinators to the flower. When an insect lands and feeds on the intoxicating liquid, it falls into the 'bucket' and its wings become wet and sticky. Because it cannot fly, the insect struggles out through a tunnel-like exit, made up of the divided labellum parts beneath the column apex, which bears the pollen. The pollen sticks to the insect as it squeezes through, and is transferred to the next flower the insect visits. Many orchid species, including the Australian *Pterostylis grandiflora*, have sensitive labella, which, when touched by even the smallest insect, spring up to the column by a reflex mechanism and imprison the pollinator, forcing it to escape through the tunnel exit. There are other variations, such as *Catasetum* Susan Fuchs (page 42), which has a stalk, or strap, by which the pollinia are attached to a sticky gland called the VISCIDIUM. It's function is to react with a trigger reflex and glue the pollen mass onto the attracted insect. *Cirrhopetalum* Elizabeth Anne 'Bucklebury' (page 19) has a labellum made up of elongated purple threads that wave in the breeze, the motion attracting pollinators. *Cirrhopetalum graveolens* (page 70) lures its pollinators, usually carrion flies, with a putrid odor smelling of rotting meat, and certain *Angraecum* species that are pollinated by moths lure them with intoxicating perfumes at night, when the moths are active. The pollination of some European *Ophrys* orchids is even more remarkable. The bizarre shapes and markings of the flowers have evolved to mimic real insects, bees, wasps, and spiders (*Ophrys kotschyi,* page 74). The English 'Bee orchid' looks extraordinarily like the female bee, and the flowers even emit a scent similar to the female in order to entice male bees. The labellum is hairy, like the female bee, and when the male lands, this deception stimulates him to copulate with the flower. In the course of this excited behavior, pollen sticks to the bee and is transferred to the next flower with which the male bee repeats his futile efforts. All of these intriguing devices add to the mystery surrounding orchids. Because many of them have evolved specifically to attract only one species of pollinator, the chances of random cross-breeding resulting in natural hybridization are reduced, ensuring the successful continuation of a species in its true form.

The great naturalist, Charles Darwin, was one of the first botanists to study the strange co-evolution between orchids and their pollinators. In certain orchids at the rear of the labellum, there can be a spur of various lengths, or a bulbous sac, often containing nectar to attract pollinators. Darwin felt there must be a logical reason why orchids evolved in this way. In his famous book *On the Various Contrivances by which British and Foreign Orchids are Fertilised by Insects*, 1862, he describes the orchid *Angraecum sesquipedale* (page 87) found in Madagascar, with a spur eleven and a half inches long, with nectar in the lower part. He predicted that an insect pollinator with a proboscis of this length would be found in the same environment. Entomologists of the time ridiculed his prediction, but in 1934 a moth was found that pollinates this orchid, and the moth was named *Xanthopan morgani* var. *'Praedicta'* to commemorate Darwin's prediction.

The OVARY is not fully developed at the time the flower opens and is hardly distinguishable from the rest of the flower stalk unless fertilization takes place. Once fertilized, the flowers quickly wither and the ovary swells and completes its formation to become a very obvious fruit or seed pod, botanically known as a 'capsule'. It is made up of three capillary sections packed with tiny seeds. The pod usually takes between six months and one year to ripen and yellow, at which point, it bursts along its fluted sides, releasing seed to be dispersed by the wind. A single pod might contain several thousand seeds, or, as in the case of *Cycnoches ventricosum var. chlorochilon* several million. The minute seeds are dust-like and as fine as face powder. They consist only of a tiny embryo, protected by a thin covering called 'testa,' and do not contain the built-in nutrient reserves to sustain the embryo, which are found in the seeds of most other flowering plants. This accounts for another characteristic of the orchid family: during the early stages of growth, orchid seeds are absolutely dependant upon a specific type of fungus called MYCORRHIZA (from the Greek for fungus root), which is present in the soil or on the bark of the host tree. The fungal hyphae penetrates the seed and enters the embryo, and the seed digests the fungal tissue and obtains sugar and other high energy nutrients, which are particularly important for the seed to germinate and develop. The fungus has the ability to manufacture these nutrients by breaking down more complex substances. This association is usually limited to a few weeks, while the first green leaves develop, but in saprophytic orchids, which produce no green leaves to assist the process of photosynthesis, this association is more permanent, and all the plant's nutrition comes through the fungus. This association is SYMBIOTIC, meaning that the orchid and fungus live together and the relationship benefits each partner. The orchid provides a home for the fungus in its roots, and in return feeds on nutrients that the fungus has derived from decaying plant and animal matter. This important factor in the life-cycle of orchids was not known in the early days of orchid cultivation, and accounts for many failures and disappointments in attempts to grow orchids from seed.

HYBRIDIZATION AND MERICLONING

The majority of commercially produced orchids are hybrids derived from *Cymbidium, Cattleya, Paphiopedilum,* and *Phalaenopsis.* Although some hybrids occur naturally, no artificial hybrids were produced until the middle of the nineteenth century. Orchid seedlings were first described in 1802, but it took many years for propagation by seed to become widespread. There are unsubstantiated reports of artificial hybrids as early as the 1830s, but it was not until Dr. John Harris, a physician at the Devon & Exeter Hospital, suggested the correct method for artificial pollination to John Dominy, the orchid grower at Veitch and Sons, that a breakthrough in orchid cultivation was made. In 1856, the first artificially produced orchid hybrid flowered. It was a cross made between *Calanthe masuca* and *Calanthe furcata,* and the resulting plant was named *Calanthe* Dominyi. This proved to be a milestone in orchid history, the forerunner of the vast orchid breeding industry. Dominy's pioneering work with hybrids put the Veitch Nursery at the forefront of the field. In the early days of hybridization, attempts were made to simulate natural growing conditions by sowing seed around the base of the mother plant, or in compost that contained some of the roots of the mother plant. This was the only known way to produce new plantlets from seed. Only a few growers were successful in getting seed to germinate without knowledge of the need for mycorrhiza fungus. As cultivation techniques improved, it was quickly discovered that the orchid family is unusually promiscuous. Not only can orchids reproduce within the same genus but, within limits, different genera can also be cross-pollinated reasonably easily to produce new, novel hybrids. Specialist orchid nurseries realized the potential of artificial hybridization to improve special characteristics of flower shape, color, and longevity, and quickly became involved with hybrid experimentation.

In the early 1900s, French botanist Noel Bernard demonstrated scientifically that orchid seed could only germinate if penetrated by a particular fungal hyphae. Subsequent developments by the German mycologist, Hans Burgeff, demonstrated that orchid seed could also be germinated in test tubes, on an agar medium, providing the mycorrhiza fungus was present. But probably the most important advance in orchid cultivation came about in 1922 when Lewis Knudsen, an American plant physiologist at Cornell University, identified the nutrients that orchids derive from their mycorrhizal association and substituted the right proportions of mineral nutrients and simple sugar in an artificial medium. The seed germinated on its own, proving that the presence of the fungus was not essential. This revolutionized orchid culture and led to laboratory techniques for propagating orchids. The nutrient formula became known as the Knudsen Formula, and by the 1930s, several hundred new hybrids were being created each year. This procedure of propagation without the fungus present is called an ASYMBIOTIC method. Until recently, it was the most common method of producing commercial orchids. In 1960, however, Professor Georges Morel of the University of Paris discovered a new propagation technique for regenerating plant tissue, called MERICLONING. Orchid plants develop tiny buds of new growth called meristems, and Morel discovered that just a few millimeters of this tissue could produce an unlimited number of new plants with identical characteristics to the original plant.

By this method of orchid propagation, a young shoot is cut from the mother plant, and several layers of tissue are removed until the meristem is exposed. This growing tip is then cut out and placed in a flask of liquid nutrient solution, which is placed on a rotary wheel or a vibrating shaker for three to four weeks of continuous agitation, during which the tissue develops into large clumps. Within another month these clumps of tissue are large enough to be cut into a further twenty or thirty pieces and separated into flasks to be agitated. This pattern can be repeated indefinitely, creating new tissue growth each time. When agitation is stopped and the clumps are transferred to a culture nutrient, they start to grow into small plantlets, which can eventually be potted.

Mericlone culture has enabled commercial growers to mass-produce high quality orchids inexpensively. By normal subdivision, a mature plant of eight or nine pseudobulbs could only be split into two or three divisions that would survive and flower, but by meristem cloning an unlimited number of new plants can be produced in a fairly short period of time.

NOMENCLATURE

THE ORGANIZATION OF ORCHID NAMES

Long orchid names can be daunting and confusing to novices, especially at orchid shows when the name on the tag is followed by a combination of letters. This is due to the fact that most plants at shows are hybrids, and the situation can be further complicated to indicate an award the plant has received, or the parentage of the hybrid.

A system has been worked out by international agreement to promote uniformity and scientific understanding of orchid names. The name of a natural species normally consists of two words in Latin. The orchid family is organized into a number of different genera. The first word signifies the generic name or genus, i.e. *Cattleya, Dendrobium, Phalaenopsis,* etc. and is shown in italic type, starting with a capital letter. The second word is usually an adjective and signifies the particular species name within that genus. The species is also shown in italic type, but starting with a small initial letter, as in *Phalaenopsis violacea* and *Anguloa clowesii.* In a single genus, *Paphiopedilum,* for instance, there may be many species, such as *Paphiopedilum bellatulum, Paphiopedilum armeniacum,* and *Paphiopedilum malipoense.* Species of the same genus are more closely related to each other than to other genera.

Hybrid names are more complex. When two natural species are cross-bred, the result is called a primary hybrid. As with the names of species, the first word of the hybrid name signifies the genus and is in italic type, starting with a capital letter. If both parents are from within the same genus, then the generic name will be followed by a designated name and this is shown in roman type with a capital letter, indicating that it is an artificial hybrid. *Masdevallia* Falcata (page 25) is a primary hybrid parented by *Masdevallia veitchiana* (page 81) and *Masdevallia coccinea* (page 57). A hybrid produced from two hybrid parents is called a complex hybrid and receives a designated name in the same manner as primary hybrids. All the offspring from a common parentage are designated with the same name even though the flowers may vary from plant to plant, and any further specimens of that same cross-ing are also given the same designated name or 'Grex' name. However, one particular cultivar from that crossing may produce outstanding flowers, and in addition to the Grex name, it can be given an individual or cultivar name, which is also shown in Roman type, beginning with a capital letter but using single quotes, as in *Phalaenopsis* Sussex Pearl 'Southern Opera'. Grex names and cultivar names must obviously be fancy names that cannot be mistaken for scientific or botanical names and must consist of between one and three words in any language.

As explained previously, orchids are very promiscuous and readily cross pollinate, not only between different species of the same genus, but also between different genera. This has further complicated orchid names. Initially intergeneric hybrid names were made up of a combination of the generic names. A *Cattleya* crossed with a *Laelia* is called a *Laeliocattleya.* It then became possible to create crosses of say three, four, or even five different genera. If a *Brassavola* was crossed with a *Laelia,* crossed with a *Cattleya,* the resulting plant became a *Brassolaeliocattleya.* Abbreviations are used, for instance, *Laeliocattleya* = *Lc.* and *Brassolaeliocattleya* = *Blc.* If more genera are involved, the names would become incomprehensible, so in order to simplify matters, it was decided by international agreement that when crosses are made of three or more genera, the new multi-generic name for the hybrid should be the name of a person distinguished in the field of orchidology, suffixed by -ara. Examples are: *Sanderara* (in commemoration of Frederick Sander) = *Odontoglossum* x *Brassia* x *Cochlioda,* and *Rothara* (in commemoration of the European benefactor, Rothschild) = *Brassavola* x *Epidendrum* x *Cattleya* x *Laelia* x *Sophronitis.* Multi-generic hybrid names are also preceded by an x, as in x *Rothara.* Recently, bi-generic crosses have produced new names such as *Miltassia* (abbreviated *Mtssa.*) = *Miltonia* x *Brassia,* and *Opsisanda* (abbreviated *Opsis.*) = *Vanda* x *Vandopsis.* Multi-generic crosses are still designated with Grex names and cultivar names. At orchid shows, there may be hybrids on display that have not yet been registered with the Royal Horticultural Society, and the names of these plants indicate the genera name followed by the parentage in parentheses.

As botanists and taxonomists continue their research, and advances are made through scientific development, it has been discovered that certain plants that have been classified in one genus for many years actually belong to another. Blueprints of chromosome numbers and generic characteristics are now possible, and various species have been reclassified and their established names have been changed. For example, *Oncidium kramerianum* (page 45) has been renamed *Psychopsis krameriana* and *Brassavola digbyana* (page 37) is now called *Rhyncholaelia digbyana*. Often, the more familiar name is placed in parenthesis as a synonym (syn.), after the new name, as in *Rhyncholaelia digbyana* (syn. *Brassavola digbyana*). In 1895, Frederick Sander introduced a system for the registration of orchid hybrids, and in 1906, he published the first *Sander's List of Orchid Hybrids*. This was followed in 1946 by the *Complete List of Orchid Hybrids*, which contained some twenty thousand names. In 1961, after Sander's death, the Royal Horticultural Society of England became responsible as the International Authority for the Registration Procedure that covers hybrids. At present the RHS is the only authority that registers the pedigree of hybrids through their Grex names, and to date some eighty thousand have been registered and the number is increasing rapidly. When plant data, parentage, and other information is received, the official hybrid name is registered and printed in the English journal, *The Orchid Review*. After many years of diligent work, all the information regarding registered hybrids has been computerized and is available through the RHS Orchid Information System. This was made possible by the collaboration of three Australian computer experts, together with the RHS, The American Orchid Society, and the Singapore Botanical Gardens. Utilizing the system, one can locate the name of a particular hybrid in a matter of moments, find out its parentage, and construct a family tree.

Awards

Plants at orchid shows are frequently recommended to receive awards by the Committee of one of the established orchid societies, and both the award and the orchid society are indicated by capital letters after the name. The awards of the Royal Horticultural Society are classified as FCC (First Class Certificate, the top honor), AM (Award Merit), HCC (Highly Commended Certificate) and a special award CCM (Certificate of Cultural Merit), which is awarded to plants of exceptional quality and condition but which are not necessarily outstanding cultivars. PC (Preliminary Commendation) is sometimes given to new hybrids that the Committee would like to see on a subsequent flowering before recommending a higher award. The American Orchid Society awards the FCC, AM, and HCC, and its own additional awards: JC/AOS (Judge's Commendation), AQ/AOS (Award of Quality), CHM/AOS (Certificate of Horticultural Merit), and CBR/AOS (Certificate of Botanical Recognition). Other orchid societies worldwide also have their own award systems, separate from the international awards. There are now over forty award-giving bodies throughout the world: the letters AOS indicate the American Orchid Society, RHS the Royal Horticultural Society, HOS the Honolulu Orchid Society, AJOS the All Japan Orchid Society, RHT the Royal Horticultural Society of Thailand, SFOS the South Florida Orchid Society, and so on.

For amateur enthusiasts and professionals alike, orchid societies and clubs are an invaluable source of information and help. The American Orchid Society was founded in 1921, and is an international non-profit organization that publishes a monthly magazine called *The AOS Bulletin*. Orchid shows are held throughout the world at most times of the year, and every three years a World Orchid Conference is staged in a different country. Orchid societies have information and schedules of shows for most areas.

SCENTED ORCHIDS

When orchids were less common, it was thought that their flowers had no fragrance. It is now known that many orchids produce a scent to attract the insects that pollinate them. Scents vary between fragrant and intoxicating perfumes and pungent, quite unpleasant odors. *Miltonioides warscewiczii* (page 54) and *Oncidium* Sharry Baby both smell very strongly of chocolate, while by contrast, *Cirrhopetalum graveolens* (page 70) gives off a smell of putrid, rotting meat. While the different scents of orchids seem quite specific, it is difficult to classify their fragrances because individuals interpret smells differently. There are further complications because some orchids are fragrant only at specific times of day, and others smell only in sunlight. Similarly, scents can vary greatly within the same species, and even smell of one thing at one time of the day and of something else at another time. Many orchids are so fragrant that a single flower can perfume an entire room.

Here is a list of popular scent interpretations:

- Scent of roses—*Phragmipedium schlimii, Miltoniopsis* (syn. *Miltonia) roezlii, Trichopilia suavis, Phalaenopsis schilleriana, Cattleya labiata, Dendrobium wardianum*
- Scent of carnations—*Oncidium lawrencianum*
- Scent of vanilla—*Vanda tricolor, Vanda suavis, Phalaenopsis lueddemanniana, Pilumna fragrans.*
- Scent of violets—*Oncidium tigrinum, Rhyncholaelia digbyana, Cymbidium sinense, Dendrobium ainsworthi, Epidendrum varicosum, Maxillaria atropurpurea*
- Scent of cinnamon—*Mormodes rolfeanum, Lycaste aromatica*, and many *Odontoglossum*
- Scent of honey—*Odontoglossum blande, Angraecum sesquipedale* (only at night), *Cattleya mossiae, Laelia anceps*
- Scent of lilac—*Zygopetalum mackayi*
- Scent of daphne—*Odontoglossum maculatum*
- Scent of coconut—*Maxillaria tenuifolia*
- Scent of freshly cut cucumber—*Sarcopodium lobbii*
- Scent of coriander—*Maxillaria venusta*
- Scent of angelica—*Epidendrum alatum*
- Scent of sandalwood—*Acineta superba, Mormodes pardinum*
- Scent of fresh fruit—*Coelogyne pandurata, Scuticaria steeli*
- Scent of bitter almonds—*Satyrium candidum, Catasetum, Mormodes*
- Scent of lemon—*Encyclia citrina, Sedirea japonica*

There are many orchids with the scent of jasmine and lily of the valley, including *Coelogyne cristata alba, Maxillaria punctata, Oncidium maculatum, Angraecum arcuatum, Dendrobium primulinum, Dendrobium palpebrae, Ondontoglossum boddarertianum, Epidendrum criniferum, Epidendrum fragrans, Neofinetia falcata, Epidendrum paniculatum,* and *Epidendrum stamfordianum.*

ORCHIDS AS CUT FLOWERS

Orchid flowers look stunning in arrangements, and cut orchid flowers are available to growers and more passive enthusiasts alike. The flowers will last a very long time providing you keep them supplied with plenty of fresh water; the stems should never be allowed to dry out. Cut flowers benefit by having a small section of the stem cut off periodically when the water is replaced. This facilitates the flowers' intake of water and will extend their lifetime in a vase. If flowers become limp, immerse the whole flower spike in tepid water for about half an hour, and this should revitalize them. If the stems become mushy or yellow, cut off the affected part and replace the water. Some orchid flowers will last for at least a month indoors if they are kept cool and occasionally misted. Also avoid placing orchid blooms near ripening fruit, vegetables, or decaying flowers, because orchids are very susceptible to ethylene gas, which is a natural by-product of ripening or decay.

Some orchid flowers such as *Phalaenopsis* (the Moth orchid) have a modern graphic appearance and look stunning as minimalist arrangements of only one flower stem, while others look best in vases or bowls with strong shapes and colors. Because most orchid stems are rigid and the flowers are top-heavy, they often fall into awkward positions. Overcome this by using a spiked metal base or 'frog' in the bottom of the vase to hold the flower in position, or use several stems together so that they support each other. Adjust the shapes and curves of the individual spikes to improve the design of your arrangement. As the flower stems are cut down and shorten in length, you may need to change the vase to retain balance and design. Good cut flowers for the house are *Paphiopedilum, Phalaenopsis, Cymbidium*, and most of the Oriental types of *Oncidium, Dendrobium*, and *Vanda*, all specially grown for the cut flower trade. These are readily available at flower shops and markets.

Lycaste skinneri var. virginaliss
(White Nun orchid)
S/I
National flower of Guatemala

ORCHIDS AS HOUSE PLANTS

Today's sophisticated heating and air conditioning systems regulate temperature so that many orchids can be successfully grown in the house, providing they receive adequate light and moisture. However, they do require care and attention. Average house temperatures, around 74°F (24°C) by day and 63–68°F (18–20°C) at night, suit many orchids. A drop in temperature at night is actually conducive to healthy plants and initiates flowering. Be sure the house is not too hot, and use a fan to create air flow. For the beginner, there are several types of orchids suitable to grow in the house that will more or less guarantee success. These are *Phalaenopsis, Paphiopedilum, Miltonia, Laelia,* and many *Oncidium.* A nursery can recommend varieties that suit the environment of your home. Since most cultivated orchids are raised in the controlled conditions of a greenhouse, they will probably receive a shock when first brought into a house. Some may lose a few leaves or drop flower buds, but if they are misted regularly around the roots, they will soon recover. They all require light, and can be placed near a window, preferably facing east, southwest, or west. Plants must not be put too close to the glass—strong, direct sunlight will burn their leaves, and in winter the significant drop in temperature could harm the plant. Windows that face south are often too hot in the summer, but if a south-facing window is the only option, give careful consideration to shading. In any case, it is best to organize some shading, and depending on the variety of orchid, a simple net curtain should suffice. If your plant does not thrive, it may just need slightly more or less light, so move it to find the position where it is most successful. Most orchids require humidity of 40–70%, a higher level than exists in most houses. Use a humidifier or create a humid micro-climate for the plants by placing them on upturned flowerpots in a shallow tray filled with gravel or pebbles. Keep the tray continuously supplied with water, regardless of whether the plants need watering. The evaporation of the water will create the humid environment essential for successful cultivation. Excess moisture from misting or watering can cause marks on the leaves, and if it becomes lodged in young growth or in the roots, it might cause rot. It is the general tendency of most beginners to overwater, when in fact, orchids will tolerate occasional dryness far better than too much water.

For cooler windowsills with temperatures of around 45°F (8–10°C), *Pleione* orchids, commonly called 'Windowsill orchids' (page 14), are reliable and give a good show. These plants are deciduous, and after they flower the leaves die down. The plant should then be kept in a cool, dry place until the next growing season.

Glass terrarium cases similar to the old Victorian Wardian cases are still popular, both in traditional and modern styles, and they create an enclosed environment that can be controlled to suit the orchids you have decided to grow. Orchids that require low light levels, such as *Paphiopedilum, Masdevallia,* and certain *Phalaenopsis* are most suitable.

Keen enthusiasts may prefer to convert a room especially for growing orchids indoors, and provide artificial lighting and heating. In these conditions orchids generally flourish and grow to superior quality because they can be consistently provided with longer periods of light, whether it is summer or winter. Not all orchids are suited to indoor culture, especially *Vanda,* which requires full light, and standard *Cymbidium,* which take up a great deal of space. There are technical guides available with instructions and advice about setting up an indoor environment, but it is advisable to first obtain information from an orchid society or commercial orchid grower.

MINIATURE ORCHIDS

Even if space is limited, you need not be denied the pleasure of growing orchids. Almost every genus has some miniature or dwarf species, and there are many small hybrids that produce beautiful and exotic blooms, yet require minimum space. Some are true miniatures, and are so small that the flowers must be seen through a magnifying glass to appreciate their intricate beauty, while others, although they are borne on small plants, produce quite large and striking flowers. The acceptable size for miniature orchids, specified by the American Orchid Society, is less than 6" (15 cm) tall, excluding the spike. Miniature orchids are available at specialist nurseries. Many of them adjust slowly to indoor conditions, and it is possible that you will experience some losses. It usually takes about six months before the plants become established, and during this transitional time it is best to water them sparingly, about once a week, and keep them near a bright window where the temperature ranges between 70–75°F (20–24°C). Popular miniatures include *Encyclia citrina, Cattleya walkeriana, Dendrobium aggregatum, Sedirea japonica, Ascocentrum* species, certain *Bulbophyllum, Maxillaria, Sophronitis coccinea, Mystacidium capense, Neofinetia falcata* (Samurai orchid), and *Trichocentrum*. Another is *Laelia milleri*, a stunning orchid with scarlet flowers, which was only discovered in 1978 in Brazil. It has now been completely eradicated in the wild because a mining operation devastated its natural habitat. *Pleurothallid* orchids including *Masdevallia*, cool growing *Dryadella, Restrepia, Porroglossum*, and *Stelis* come from high up in the Andes, where there are cool, even temperatures and high humidity year round. These are popular for growing cases because of their small size, but are probably more suited to greenhouses because of the high humidity they require. Give them shady conditions with no direct sunlight.

Masdevallia veitchiana
S/C

ORCHIDS IN THE GARDEN

In temperate regions of the United States—California, Florida and Hawaii—it is possible to grow orchids outside in the garden landscape. Certain orchids can be grown directly in the ground, but they require loose, well drained soil, and it is usually preferable to grow them in pots. The hardy terrestrial species *Bletilla striata* is one of the most reliable orchids for warm, open situations, and *Laelia anceps* is easy to grow and flower. *Epidendrum radicans* also does particularly well throughout the summer. Others, such as *Cymbidium,* have a fuller, leafy appearance and are more suited to pots and containers, which can be moved about to accentuate certain shaded parts of the garden or patio. In regions where the summer is short, or the weather changeable, orchids are best left in their containers so they can be moved to shelter if the weather becomes unfavorable. Do not take orchids from the house or greenhouse straight outside to bright sunlight. Start them off in a shaded area for a few days, and then move them into dappled sunlight. Eventually they can be moved into an area that gets direct sunlight, but only during the cooler parts of the day. The best outdoor location for orchids is in a sheltered area that gets some sun. Orchids benefit from natural air currents and rain, but during dry weather they will need supplemental watering. Epiphytic plants do best with frequent spraying if conditions are dry. The following orchids are suitable for growing outside in warmer regions, during months when the temperature does not fall below 50°F (10°C), and will provide an exotic splash of color: *Aerides* species, *Brassia* species, *Cattleya* hybrids, *Dendrobium* species and hybrids, *Epidendrum* species and hybrids, *Miltonia* hybrids, and certain *Odontoglossum*, and *Oncidium*.

In cooler regions with temperatures reaching no higher than 77°F (25°C) during the day, it is possible to grow terrestrial orchids, many of which are hardy, and generally flower between spring and summer. A location facing south or east is best. *Cypripedium* and *Calanthe* enjoy cool and comparatively shady conditions. They demand well-drained soil and plenty of moisture, combined with a cool atmosphere. The North American species of *Cypripedium* do well in open situations, and in Europe certain *Dactylorhiza* and *Ophrys* flourish in lawns providing the grass is not cut early in the year, and they can be left in the ground over winter. Most terrestrial orchids originate in woodland conditions and thrive in semi-shade and well-drained, moisture-retentive soil. Certain *Pleione* species from China and the Himalayas will even flower in areas that have a few degrees of frost and are best planted in the shade of a tree or in a rockery. For conservation reasons, it is important to buy these plants from specialist growers, and not to collect them from the wild.

GROWING ORCHIDS
IN THE GREENHOUSE

More serious hobbyists will eventually decide to house their collection of plants, and most hobbyists growing orchids in the controlled conditions of a greenhouse can obtain excellent results. Commercially grown orchids are generally cultivated in greenhouses, and today their cultivation is comparatively simple. Modern hybrids have evolved from nearly a century of breeding and are more vigorous. Before purchasing plants, it is important to consider what conditions you are able to provide, and to make sure they are suitable for the orchids you wish to grow. Although most orchids require a temperature range consistent with their place of origin, they can almost all be accommodated within three temperature climates: Cool House, Intermediate House, and Hot House. Some enthusiasts derive great satisfaction from growing only one particular genus, and this makes providing suitable conditions easier. However, if you intend to grow a range of orchids, a number of different environments must be provided. The most successful greenhouses recreate the atmosphere of moist air, bright, filtered light, and moderate temperature of forests and intermediate altitudes in the tropics. The purpose of a greenhouse is not only to provide a suitable growing environment, but also to protect plants from excessive heat, dry atmosphere, and excessive light.

COOL HOUSE

The cool house is meant to reproduce the conditions of cooler temperate zones or high altitude areas in the tropics where temperatures drop at night. The night temperature should not drop below 50°F (10°C). The daytime temperature is equally important, and should not exceed 75–77°F (24–25°C). In the cool house, it is more of a problem to keep the temperature down than up, and it will probably be necessary to provide shade in the form of netting, so that the midday sun does not create temperatures that are too high. If you live in a temperate zone, it is possible to overcome this problem by putting certain orchids outside, or by opening a ventilator. A distinct drop in nighttime temperature is required for cool-growing orchids to flower. Orchids ideal for the cool house are:

Cymbidium, Calanthe, high altitude *Coelogyne* species, *Disa*, some *Dendrobium, Masdevallia, Maxillaria*, cool-growing *Odontoglossum* (both species and hybrids), cool-growing *Paphiopedilum* (Slipper orchids), *Zygopetalum, Oncidium*, and European terrestrials including *Ophrys, Dactylorhiza*, and *Orchis* .

INTERMEDIATE OR TEMPERATE HOUSE

This environment probably suits the widest range of orchids, and is meant to reproduce warmer sub-tropical areas. The night temperature should not drop below 55–60°F (13–15°C) and the daytime temperature should not exceed 75–80°F (24–27°C). This section could easily be a partitioned part of your cool greenhouse, and would greatly increase the range of orchids you could grow. Orchids ideal for the intermediate house are: *Cattleya* and related genera, *Miltonia*, certain *Calanthe*, certain *Paphiopedilum*. many *Dendrobium, Huntleya alliance*, and *Oncidium*.

HOT HOUSE (STOVE HOUSE)

The hot house, occasionally called the warm house, is meant to reproduce tropical zones and jungle conditions. The night temperature should not drop below 65–68°F (18–20°C) and the daytime temperature can rise to 80–85°F (27–29°C). Orchids in this climate generally require a humid atmosphere which can be achieved by regularly spraying a bed of pebbles or felt. Overhead misting is not recommended. They also require good ventilation to prevent standing moisture from rotting the roots. It is the general rule that as temperature rises, ventilation should be increased, but beware of the associated temperature drop if a window is opened. One can grow some of the most spectacular orchids in hot house conditions. Orchids ideal for the hot house are: warm-growing *Calanthe*, heat-loving and lowland *Dendrobium* species and hybrids, most *Phalaenopsis* (Moth orchid) species, and most *Vanda* and Vandaceous types, including *Ascocenda*.

GENERAL CULTIVATION

TEMPERATURE AND HEATING

In these three greenhouse environments it is essential to have the heating system set to create a contrast between day and night temperatures. Most orchids require a temperature drop of between 10–15°F (-12– -9°C) at night in order to flower. Heat can be provided either by a hot air heater or by piped hot water, but the latter is usually better because the relatively large surface area of the pipework ensures that heat is distributed evenly throughout the greenhouse and does not dry the air. Pipework is best situated below the growing benches. Be sure that fumes from fuel-generated heaters are vented externally.

HUMIDITY

Most tropical orchids originate in environments with high humidity all year round, even in regions where there is a distinct cycle of wet and dry seasons. In rainforests, the humidity is maintained by regular rainfall, coupled with warm temperatures. All orchids thrive in a relatively humid atmosphere and this can be achieved in greenhouses either by damping down floors or benches or by using an automatic humidifier. Generally, the humidity balance should vary with the temperature; when the temperature is high, the humidity level should be equally high, and when the temperature drops, the humidity can be lower. For this reason, high humidity is more important in the summer. Beware of damp conditions overnight in cool weather, because this can create an environment conducive to fungal and bacterial disease and rotting.

LIGHT AND SHADING

Adequate light is of prime importance for the health of orchids and their capacity to produce flowers. Orchids with leaves generally function through photosynthesis, and cannot flower without sufficient light. However, some orchids such as *Paphiopedilum* are forest or jungle ground dwellers and grow in the shade. These plants need to be given special consideration, and nearly all orchids benefit from some form of diffused shading. Netting, mesh, or even white paint on the outside of the glass are all appropriate and will give optimum light levels, keeping temperatures down in summer. It is a good idea to provide an area in which shading has been adjusted for more light-sensitive plants. *Phalaenopsis* types, for instance, require heavier shade than *Vanda*. The general aim is to keep the light level up to the optimum—decrease shading during the shorter days of winter.

VENTILATION

In their natural habitat, there is always some air movement around orchids, either by convection from the forest floor or from breezes. Most orchids benefit from air circulation, and it is advisable to operate a small fan twenty-four hours a day. This will help to eliminate any pockets of stagnant air, particularly in corners, where mold and fungi might otherwise tend to develop. Orchids will not grow in stagnant air. A pleasant, airy atmosphere, whether in the cool, intermediate, or hot house, is a sign of healthy plants. Be careful of any direct drafts, which can cause plants to drop their flower buds, stunt growth, or make plants prone to disease.

CONTAINERS

The majority of orchids, whether epiphytic or terrestrial, are normally sold in flower pots (usually plastic or clay) like other house plants. Always make sure these pots have abundant drain holes. Epiphytic orchids with long and vigorous root growth such as *Vanda* are normally grown in wooden or plastic baskets. Those with pendulous flower growth, such as *Stanhopea* and *Coryanthes*, are sold in wooden or metal baskets lined with moss or peat, so that the inflorescence can grow downwards. Miniature orchids and smaller types are often mounted on cork or oak bark, giving a much better idea of how orchids grow naturally in the wild. However, they are generally more manageable and reliable in pots.

COMPOSTS

When deciding on a compost mix for your orchid, it is important to consider the plant's requirements in terms of whether it is epiphytic or terrestrial, and the fineness of its root system.

Most tropical orchids are epiphytes and grow on trees in the wild. Their roots cling to the bark surface of host trees and are often in contact with a shallow layer of moss and ferns. Rainwater passes through the root system very quickly, then dries out. Commercially, efforts are made to recreate these conditions by growing orchids in loose, coarse compost so that water can pass through the root system rapidly, allowing air to permeate the compost soon after watering. The air spaces are important for good root development. Orchids thrive in a wide range of growing mediums, but the most common composts consist of milled or chopped pine, fir bark chips, redwood fiber, sphagnum moss, or coconut husks. Usually Perlite or lumpy peat moss is added for extra water retention. All composts tend to break down eventually, so many growers extend the life of the mix by using inert fillers such as charcoal, rockwool, or volcanic scoria (scree), which are slow to decay. The nutrient supply of compost mixes is not important because most orchids in cultivation are supplemented with liquid fertilizer during their growth season.

Terrestrial orchids generally originate in woodland areas, and an open, humus-rich soil that keeps the roots well aerated is best. Use a finer compost than with epiphytes. A loam-based mix will retain more moisture.

WATERING

Orchids require two types of watering—on the roots, and around the plant in the form of humidity. When considering the water requirements of your particular orchid, you must consider its natural origin. Plants that come from regions with specific wet and dry seasons need to be kept moist during their growing period in spring and summer. During the rest period in winter, they require less water, just enough to prevent shriveling and dehydration. Other orchids come from climates that are reasonably constant throughout the year, and these plants require water most of the time, although generally less during the winter. To water potted plants, plenty of water should be poured into the pot, until the water floods through and runs out of the drainholes. Allow time for excess water to drain. During the growth period this should be done every four to seven days, and during the rest period, every five to eight days. Terrestrial orchids in loam-based composts require a more even watering regime. During their growth period,

they should not be allowed to dry out as much as epiphytes. Experience will best tell you how frequently to water, but a good indication is to lift the whole pot. If the compost is dry and the plant needs water, it will feel distinctly light and top-heavy. If there is any doubt, wait until the next day. The pot must not be allowed to stand in excess water, which will rot the roots and encourage disease.

Orchids mounted on bark require moisture more regularly than those in pots or containers, because their roots tend to be exposed, and quickly dry out. Spray the plant frequently, especially around the roots, or dunk the lower part of the plant into a bucket of tepid water once a day.

Do not water with tap water unless the salt content is less than three hundred parts per million. You can check this level with your water authority. If water is heavily chlorinated, either filter it through a reverse osmosis unit or use rainwater.

FEEDING

In the wild, orchids have adapted to nutrient-poor habitats, and rely only on nutrients from decaying organic matter. They are slow growers and require less food than most other plants. However, because there are few nutrients in modern composts, feeding is essential. Any balanced liquid feed or soluble fertilizer is adequate providing it is given on a regular basis. Use fertilizer diluted to one-third or one-half of the normal strength used for other plants. Orchids need nutrients to stimulate growth, and to produce foliage, flowers, and seed. It is best to add fertilizer every other watering during the growth period, and every three waterings when the plant is dormant.

REPOTTING

Orchids require repotting on a regular basis, normally every one or two years, either when the plant has outgrown its container, or when the compost has deteriorated. Epiphytic orchids require fresh compost every year. The best time for repotting is when new roots emerge, usually in the spring. Sympodial orchids, which grow along rhizome stems should be repotted when new roots emerge from the base of the previous years' growth. Monopodial orchids such as *Vanda* and *Ascocenda* should be repotted when new growth shows at the growing tip and there is new root growth.

To repot epiphytes, remove the plant from its old container, taking care not to damage foliage and roots, and discard the old compost. Cut off any dead or diseased roots, which look dried out or mushy, with a sterilized knife. (You can sterilize a knife by holding the blade over the flame from a burner or stove.) Be sure that no secretion is transferred from one plant to another to avoid spreading viral disease. Gently strip away dead or diseased foliage, and clean pseudobulbs of any ragged fibre. Check that you have chosen a suitable pot in relation to both the size of the plant and the amount of healthy roots. Make sure that the end result will not be top-heavy and fall over. If you are using a plastic pot, an alternative is to use a terra-cotta pot which will be heavier. For good drainage, use pots with abundant drain holes. Place pottery shards in the base of the pot, and cover them with compost. Position the plant sensibly in the pot so there is room for new growth. Plants with growth all around need to be centered, while others that grow forward, such as *Cattleya*, need to be positioned to one side with the old growth against the edge of the pot. Most rhizome plants should be placed above the surface. Pour compost all around the roots, leaving no gaps, and fill the pot to the top. Tap the pot against a hard surface to settle the compost, and press lightly on top to secure the plant. Stake the plant if it bends or leans.

The general principle for repotting terrestrials is virtually the same as for epiphytes. However, it is important that a quantity of the old compost containing the mycorrhizal fungus should be transposed over to the new mix. About twenty-five percent will ensure that the fungus is present. Repot the plant when it comes into new growth. Dormant species whose foliage dies down in winter should be repotted in early spring. Rhizomes and tubers of terrestrial orchids should be placed about 1" to 1½" (2.5–4 cm) below the surface of the compost.

Some epiphytic orchids such as *Encyclia citrina* have a natural habit of downward growth, and do not fit well into standard pots. Miniatures and many others often look best displayed in a more natural way. An alternative to potting is to mount them on a piece of bark or length of branch and hang them up. You can buy cork pieces especially for the purpose, but native oak is an excellent substitute. Whatever you choose, it should be a hardwood that will not rot, and should ideally be seasoned for six to twelve months. Place a small pad of organic matter, either fern fibre or moss, between the plant and the bark before securing it. This will absorb extra moisture and provide a reservoir around the roots. Tie the plant to the bark or branch using an inert material such as fishing line or plastic-coated wire. Bear in mind that this method of culture requires more time and attention in terms of watering and humidity, and plants will require regular misting both on the foliage and at the roots so they will not dry out.

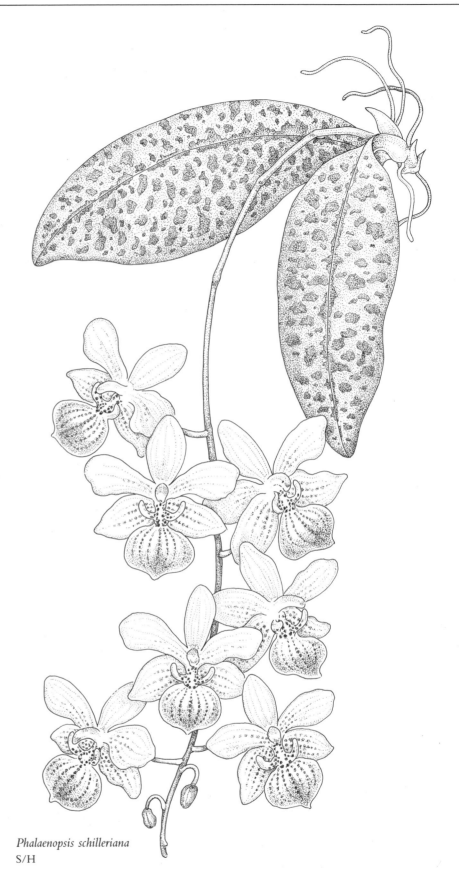

Phalaenopsis schilleriana
S/H

DIVISION OF PLANTS

Orchid plants can be divided if they are too large for their pots, or if multiple plants are desired. In the case of sympodial orchids with pseudobulbs, division is similar to the division of other herbaceous plants. For best results, orchids should be divided when new roots are emerging, usually in the spring, as they are being repotted. To make sure a subdivision is feasible, the proposed new plant should consist of a growing shoot with at least two years' growth behind it, but a good size new division should consist of about four pseudobulbs. With a sharp, sterile knife, make a clean cut through the creeping rhizoneous stem at the base of the plant between the pseudobulbs. Pot the subdivision separately, placing the older growth at the edge of the pot, leaving the new growth in the center with room for it to grow forward. Repot the old back-bulbs separately; they should produce new growth from the dormant "eye" at the base of the pseudobulb, and will also flower in due course.

In the case of certain sympodial orchids, such as *Dendrobium,* the pseudobulbs are cane-like and can be propagated by cuttings. After the plant has flowered, cut an old stem into sections, each with several leaf nodes. Lay the cuttings on sphagnum felt or moss and keep it moist and shaded. In due course new plant growth will develop from most cuttings.

Monopodial orchids cannot be divided by these methods. When Vandaceous types grow to a considerable height, roots emerge at random points on the upper stem, and it is possible to cut off the top section of the stem to create a new growing plant. Use a sterile knife and make a clean diagonal cut, making sure that the top section consists of a piece of stem with three or more pairs of leaves below the growing tip and has active roots so that the new plant can absorb moisture and nutrients. Once the growing tip has been removed, the old remaining stump will quickly send up suckers, and these should eventually develop into flowering plants. Many monopodial orchids also develop young plants from their base, or from any point on the stem, especially if the growing tip has been damaged. These can be cut off and potted.

Some orchids, such as *Dendrobium* and *Phalaenopsis* types, produce small plantlets called KEIKIS (from the Hawaiian, meaning baby). These can grow from the nodes of pseudobulbs, sometimes from the "eyes," and sometimes even from the flower spikes. When they have developed their own roots, the plantlets can be removed with a sterile knife and potted separately.

Spring is the best time to make plant divisions. It is the period of new growth, and gives the greatest span of time for healing and regrowth before the dormant period in fall or winter. It is important to remember not to divide plants at random unless you specifically want to increase your plant collection. During the time that it takes for a new subdivision to flower, the original plant could have matured and perhaps become an award-winning plant covered in bloom.

It is also possible to build up your collection by buying young plants, which are relatively inexpensive. With mericloned plants, one can guarantee the characteristics of the flower. If the seedlings are very small, they will initially require more humid conditions, and as they become established, they can be potted individually and placed in normal greenhouse conditions.

PESTS AND DISEASES

Orchids can be affected by the same pests and diseases that attack other plants, but prompt action will usually cure any problems. The most common pests are aphids, mealy bugs, and scale. These can all be treated with commercial remedies from a nursery, or by applying standard alcohol or methylated spirits on a cotton swab to the affected areas. Repeat treatment may be required. Red spider mites are another common pest, and can be treated with an appropriate miticide. It is now also possible to obtain a range of natural predators direct from the nursery to control most common pests.

Fungal and bacterial diseases may attack orchids, and usually affect weakened plants. The risk is greatly reduced if new plant stock is healthy. Disease is manifested in powdery, mushy foliage growth, often with dark, mottled staining around the affected areas. The cause is usually bad cultivation practices— the result of excessive moisture when the weather is damp and cold, insufficient heating or ventilation, or excessive humidity, all of which create the stagnant conditions under which bacteria thrive. Contaminated water is also a common cause of disease, and the water supply container should be inspected frequently for mold or slime. Check the plants' roots for waterlogging or rot, and get advice from an orchid specialist. If spraying is recommended, avoid getting liquid insecticides on the flower buds, because this can damage them. When spraying, be careful not to get chemical treatments on your skin. Use gloves, and always wear goggles. Only mix the quantity you require for immediate use, and store chemicals in a locked cabinet or on a high shelf, out of the reach of children.

Viruses, which manifest themselves in whithering or mottling, are usually spread by mechanical means, such as a grower using an infected knife. Viruses are systemic, and can kill or disfigure plants very quickly. There are no remedies, and infected plants cannot be cured. If plants are infected, they should be removed immediately from the greenhouse and destroyed or isolated.

ORCHID CONSERVATION

All of today's orchids, both species and hybrids, were originally derived from wild orchids, which once flourished in their natural habitats in many parts of the world. While many of these still remain, others are under threat and are decreasing in number. Certain tropical habitats have been destroyed through logging and oil extraction for commercial gain, and in these habitats, many natural orchid species have perished. Because of this destruction, and also through alteration of habitat by pollution and contamination, it is estimated that one-third of all natural orchid species will be threatened with extinction over the next twenty-five years. Fortunately, this problem has received a great deal of publicity, and more recently specific action has been taken to protect orchids and other rare plants.

In many countries, legislation has been introduced to protect wild orchids, and nature reserves and protected areas have been established to give them a chance to survive. In this endeavor, it is best to boycott the purchase of native plants that have been collected from the wild. In 1975, the import and export of orchids became controlled through a treaty drawn up by the Convention of International Trade in Endangered Species of Wild Fauna and Flora (CITES), and this legislation has been adopted by over one hundred countries. International trade in orchids between signatories of the agreement must be accompanied by appropriate CITES export documents. Since 1992, however, all orchid seedlings in flasks are exempt, because they are artificially cultivated.

In populated regions also, where new towns and cities are being established, the boundaries of wild areas are decreasing and native orchids are becoming endangered. In the United States, endemic orchid species including *Calypso, Calopogon, Cypripedium, Epipactis,* and *Habenaria* are threatened. In England, there is only one known specimen of *Cypripedium calceolus* (Yellow Lady's Slipper orchid) left in the wild, and many species of *Ophrys* are endangered. Much thought has been given to the problem of areas destined for destruction or development, and specialists are sometimes encouraged to collect wild orchids before development is allowed to proceed. Today, fortunately, many threatened orchids are being cultivated by experienced growers and re-introduced into the wild. Mericlone techniques have been utilized to regenerate certain rare orchids, albeit in the laboratory, but this work is keeping them from extinction.

It is encouraging to note that new orchid species are still being discovered. *Phragmipedium besseae* (page 24), the only Slipper orchid with scarlet coloring, was discovered in Peru in 1981, despite the location of its habitat adjacent to a main thoroughfare. *Paphiopedilum armeniacum* (page 68) from southern China was also recently introduced. With the opening of the eastern block countries, even more species are coming to light and expeditions to remote tropical regions continue to make new discoveries.

Conservation of the world's natural resources is now a major global issue, and there is a common effort to achieve a more practical and efficient progress. We must take appropriate action now to protect the world's wild places and maintain a proper balance of nature. The mysterious and alluring orchid has evolved and adapted throughout its long history to ensure its own survival if its habitat is not destroyed. Thousands of enthusiasts all over the world have discovered the challenge of growing these beautiful flowers, and the importance of preserving their presence in nature for future generations to discover.

LIST OF SOCIETIES AND SUPPLIERS

AMERICAN ORCHID SOCIETIES

The American Orchid Society
6000 South Olive Street
West Palm Beach, FL 33405

Telephone: 407-585-8666
Fax: 407-585-0654

The AOS has over 400 affiliated
societies in every region of the
United States. To request the
name and address of a society in
your area, or to join the AOS as
a member, call or write to the
address above.

AMERICAN ORCHID SUPPLIERS

The Angraecum House
10385 East Drive
Grass Valley, CA 95945

A & P Orchids
110 Peters Road
Swansea, MA 02777

Bergstrom Orchids
494 Camino Manzanas
Thousand Oaks, CA 91360

Cal-Orchid Inc.
1251 Orchid Drive
Santa Barbara, CA 93111

Carmela Orchids, Inc.
P.O. Box H
Hakalau, HI 96710

Carter & Holmes, Inc.
#1 Mendenhall Road
Newberry, SC 29108

Creole Orchids
P.O. Box 24458
New Orleans, LA 70184

Everglades Orchids
1101 Tabit Rd.
Belle Glade, FL 33430

Hillsview Gardens
22714 S.E. Borges Road
Gresham, OR 97080

H & R Nurseries
41–240 Hihimanu Street
Waimanalo, HI 96795

J and L Orchids
20 Sherwood Road
Easton, CT 06612

Kawamoto Orchid Nursery
2630 Waiomao Rd.
Honolulu, HI 96816

Kensington Orchids
3301 Plyers Mill Road
Kensington, MD 20895

Lines Orchids
1823 Taft Highway
Signal Mountain, TN 37377

Orchid Art
1433 Kew Avenue
Hewlett, NY 11557

Orchids and Ferns
7820 Bellaire Boulevard
Houston, TX 77036

Orchids by Hausermann, Inc.
2N 134 Addison Road
Villa Park, IL 60181

Orchids de Oro
3077 S. La Cienega Boulevard
Culver City, CA 90232

Orchids Limited
4630 N. Fernbrook Lane
Plymouth, MN 55446

Orchid World International, Inc.
10885 SW 95th Street
Miami, FL 33176

Owens Orchids
18 Orchidheights Drive
Pisgah, NC 28768

Penn Valley Orchids
239 Old Gulph Road
Wynnewood, PA 19096

Richella Orchids
2881 Booth Rd.
Honolulu, HI 96813

R.F. Orchids, Inc.
28100 SW182nd Ave.
Homestead, FL 33030

Riverbend Orchids
14220 Lorraine Road
Biloxi, MS 39532

Rod McLellan Co.
1450 El Camino Real
San Francisco, CA 94080

Stewart Orchids, Inc.
3376 Foothill Road
P.O. Box 550
Carpinteria, CA 93014

Taylor Orchids
3022 Bluebush
Monroe, MI 48161

Waldor Orchids, Inc.
10 E. Poplar Avenue
Linwood, NJ 08221

Yamamoto Dendrobiums Hawaii
P.O. Box 235
Mountain View, HI 96771

Zuma Canyon Orchids, Inc.
5949 Bonsall Drive
Malibu, CA 90265

CANADIAN ORCHID SOCIETIES

American Orchid Society
6000 South Olive Street
West Palm Beach, FL 33405

Telephone: 407-585-8666
Fax: 407-585-0654

Many Canadian orchid societies
are affiliated with the AOS. To
request the name and address of
a society in your area, or to join
the AOS as a member, call or
write at the address above.

CANADIAN ORCHID SUPPLIERS

Clargreen Gardens Limited
814 Southdown Road
Mississauga, ONTARIO L5J 2Y4

Fieldwick Orchid Company
RR #1
Morpeth, ONTARIO N0P 1X0

Huronview Nurseries & Garden Centre
1811 Brigden Road
Brights Grove, ONTARIO N0N 1C0

Kilworth Orchids
RR #3
Komoka, ONTARIO N0L 1R0

Orchid Haven
900 Rossland Road E
Whitby, ONTARIO L1N 5R5

Orchids North
7005 Brentwood Drive
Brentwood Bay, BRITISH
COLUMBIA V0S 1A0

Orchiflora, Inc.
7650 Naples
Brossard, QUEBEC J4Y 1E1

Poul Hansen Orchids
4980 Echo Drive
Victoria, BRITISH COLUMBIA
V8X 3X3

Schen-Dare Orchids
3225 50th Avenue
Lloydminster, SASKATCHEWAN
S9V 0N8

BRITISH ORCHID SOCIETIES

ROYAL HORTICULTURAL
SOCIETY
Vincent Square
London SW1P 2PE

Telephone: 71 834 4333
For membership: 71 821 3000

THE BIRMINGHAM ORCHID
SOCIETY
26 Halesowen Road
West Midlands B62 9AA

THE BRITISH ORCHID
GROWERS' ASSOCIATION
Plested Orchids
38 Florence Road
College Town, Camberley
Surrey GU15 4QD

THE BOURNEMOUTH ORCHID
SOCIETY
11 Lacon Close
Bitterne Park
Southampton SO2 4JA

THE BRISTOL AND WEST OF
ENGLAND ORCHID SOCIETY
'Vron', Bath Road
Leonard Stanley, Stonehouse
Gloucestershire GL10 3LR

THE CHELTENHAM AND
DISTRICT ORCHID SOCIETY
15 Lapwing Close
Northway, Tewkesbury
Gloucestershire GL20 8TN

THE CHESHIRE AND NORTH
WALES ORCHID SOCIETY
31 Windermere Road
Birkenhead
Merseyside L43 9SJ

THE COTSWOLD AMATEUR
ORCHID SOCIETY
26 Beverston
Tetbury
Gloucestershire GL8 8TT

THE CUMBRIA ORCHID
SOCIETY
'Stanegate', Newcastle Road
Brampton
Cumbria CA8 1ES

THE DEVON ORCHID SOCIETY
Willand Post Office
Willand Old Village
Cullompton, Devon EX15 2RJ

THE EAST ANGLIA ORCHID
SOCIETY
38 Church Meadow
Alpington
Norwich NR14 7NY

THE EAST MIDLANDS ORCHID
SOCIETY
28 Merleswen
Dunholme
Lincoln LN2 3ST

THE ERIC YOUNG ORCHID
FOUNDATION
Victoria Village, Trinity
Jersey JE3 5HH

FENLAND ORCHID SOCIETY
50 Sunningdale
Orfen Waterville
Peterborough PE2 0UB

HARROGATE ORCHID SOCIETY
11 Templestowe Hill
Leeds LS15 7EJ

THE NORTHEAST OF ENGLAND
ORCHID SOCIETY
36 Harthope Close, Rickleton
Washington
Tyne & Wear NE38 9DZ

THE NORTH OF ENGLAND
ORCHID SOCIETY
8 Hartington Road, Bramhill
Stockport
Cheshire SK7 2 DZ

THE NORTH HAMPSHIRE
ORCHID SOCIETY
6 Ashworth Drive, The Ridings
Thatcham Moors, Thatcham
Berks RG3 4UU

THE ORCHID SOCIETY OF
GREAT BRITAIN
'Athelney', 145 Binscombe Village
Godalming
Surrey GU7 3QL

THE SCOTTISH ORCHID
SOCIETY
2 Carlingnose Court
North Queensferry
Fife KY11 1EP

SHEFFIELD AND DISTRICT
ORCHID SOCIETY
24 Park Vale Drive
Thryburgh
Rotherham S65 4HZ

THE SOLIHULL AND DISTRICT
ORCHID SOCIETY
84 Forge Mill Road
Redditch
Worchestershire B98 8HG

THE SOUTHERN COUNTIES
ORCHID SOCIETY
109 Foredown Drive
Portslade, Brighton
Sussex BN41 2BF

THE SOUTHEAST ORCHID
SOCIETY
33 Albany Road
Capel-le-Ferne
Folkstone
Kent CT18 7LA

SOUTHWEST ORCHID SOCIETY
'Freshwater', Bull Street
Creech St. Michael
Taunton
Somerset TA3 5PW

THE SOMERSET ORCHID
SOCIETY
'Sunrays', Newtown
West Pennard
Glastonbury
Somerset BA6 8NL

SWINDON ORCHID SOCIETY
85 Crawford Close
Freshbrook
Swindon
Wiltshire SN5 8PR

THE THAMES VALLEY ORCHID
SOCIETY
45 Thorncliffe Road
Oxford OX2 7BA

THE WESSEX ORCHID SOCIETY
'Helvellyn', 4 Southampton Road
Fareham
Hampshire PO16 7DY

THE WEST CORNWALL ORCHID
SOCIETY
St. Martins Villa, 13 Pendarves Road
Camborne
Cornwall TR14 7QB

THE WILTSHIRE ORCHID
SOCIETY
1 Rock Lane
Warminster
Wiltshire BA12 9JZ

THE WORCESTERSHIRE
ORCHID SOCIETY
47 Bruce Road
Kidderminster
Worcestershire DY10 2TX

BRITISH ORCHID SUPPLIERS

BURNHAM NURSERIES LTD and
ORCHID PARADISE
Forches Cross
Newton Abbot
Devon TQ12 6PZ

BUTTERFIELDS PLEIONES
Harvest Hill
Bourne End
Buckinghamshire SL8 5JJ

DAVID STEAD ORCHIDS
Langley Farm, Westgate Lane
Lofthouse
Wakefield WF3 3PA

DEVA ORCHIDS
Littlebrook Farm, Stryt Isa
Pen-y-ffordd
Chester CH4 0JY

EQUATORIAL PLANT CO.
7 Gray Lane
Barnard Castle
Co Durham DL12 8PD

GREENAWAY ORCHIDS
Rookery Farm, Puxton
Nr Weston-super-Mare
Avon BS24 6TL

IVENS ORCHIDS
'Great Barn Dell'
St. Albans Road
Sandridge, St. Albans
Hertfordshire AL4 9LB

MANSELL & HATCHER LTD.
Cragg Wood Nurseries
Woodlands Drive
Rawdon
Leeds LS19 6LQ

ORCHID SUNDRIES LTD.
New Gate Farm
Scotchey Lane
Stour Provost
Gillingham
Dorset SP8 5LT

PHOENIX ORCHIDS
Pennine House
Pinnar Lane
Southowram
Halifax HX3 9QT

PLESTED ORCHIDS
38 Florence Road
College Town, Camberley
Surrey GU15 4QD

RATCLIFFE ORCHIDS LTD.
Owslebury
Winchester
Hampshire SO21 1LR

ROYDEN ORCHIDS
Perks Lane, Prestwood
Gt. Missenden
Buckinghamshire HP16 0JD

STONEHURST NURSERIES
Ardingly
Sussex RH17 6TN

WOODSTOCK ORCHIDS &
AUTOMATION DIVISION
Woodstock House, 50 Pound Hill
Great Brickhill
Nr. Milton Keynes MK17 9AS

WHITMOOR HOUSE ORCHID
NURSERY
Whitmoor House, Ashill
Cullompton
Devon EX15 3NP

AUSTRALIAN ORCHID SOCIETIES

American Orchid Society
6000 South Olive Street
West Palm Beach, FL 33405

Telephone: 407-585-8666
Fax: 407-585-0654

Many Australian orchid societies
are affiliated with the AOS. To
request the name and address of
a society in your area, or to join
the AOS as a member, call or
write at the address above.

AUSTRALIAN ORCHID SUPPLIERS

Lonne's Nursery
15 Hoad Street
Earlville, Qld.
Australia

Royale Orchids
42 Pratley Street
Woywoy, NSW 2256
Australia